T0328192

Cambridge Elements ≡

Elements in Phonetics
edited by
David Deterding
Universiti Brunei Darussalam

PHONETICS IN THE BRAIN

Pelle Söderström
Lund University
Western Sydney University

CAMBRIDGE
UNIVERSITY PRESS

Shaftesbury Road, Cambridge CB2 8EA, United Kingdom

One Liberty Plaza, 20th Floor, New York, NY 10006, USA

477 Williamstown Road, Port Melbourne, VIC 3207, Australia

314–321, 3rd Floor, Plot 3, Splendor Forum, Jasola District Centre, New Delhi – 110025, India

103 Penang Road, #05–06/07, Visioncrest Commercial, Singapore 238467

Cambridge University Press is part of Cambridge University Press & Assessment, a department of the University of Cambridge.

We share the University's mission to contribute to society through the pursuit of education, learning and research at the highest international levels of excellence.

www.cambridge.org
Information on this title: www.cambridge.org/9781009507448

DOI: 10.1017/9781009161114

First published 2024

A catalogue record for this publication is available from the British Library.

ISBN 978-1-009-50744-8 Hardback
ISBN 978-1-009-16112-1 Paperback
ISSN 2634-1689 (online)
ISSN 2634-1670 (print)

Phonetics in the Brain

Elements in Phonetics

DOI: 10.1017/9781009161114
First published online: March 2024

Pelle Söderström
Lund University
Western Sydney University
Author for correspondence: Pelle Söderström, pelle.soderstrom@ling.lu.se

Abstract: Spoken language is a rapidly unfolding signal: a complex code that the listener must crack to understand what is being said. From the structures of the inner ear through to higher-order areas of the brain, a hierarchy of interlinked processes transforms the acoustic signal into a linguistic message within fractions of a second. This Element outlines how speech is perceived and explores what the auditory system needs to achieve to make this possible. It traces a path through the system and discusses the mechanisms that enable us to perceive speech as a coherent sequence of words. This is combined with a brief history of research into language and the brain beginning in the nineteenth century, as well as an overview of the state-of-the-art neuroimaging and analysis techniques that are used to investigate phonetics in the brain today. This title is also available as Open Access on Cambridge Core.

Keywords: phonetics, neurolinguistics, speech perception, psycholinguistics, neuroscience

ISBNs: 9781009507448 (HB), 9781009161121 (PB), 9781009161114 (OC)
ISSNs: 2634-1689 (online), 2634-1670 (print)

Contents

1 Introduction

Our capacity to understand spoken language is remarkable. We achieve this seemingly with ease through complex and overlapping processes that take a continuous acoustic signal as input, leading to the perception of speech sounds and coherent speech; prosodic features such as rhythm, stress, and intonational contours and categories; discrete words and, ultimately, meaning.

Speech unfolds over time, often in challenging circumstances such as busy streets or noisy restaurants, at rates of 10–15 phonemes per second (Studdert-Kennedy, 1987), with the sound signal only available for 50–100 milliseconds in auditory memory (Elliott, 1962; Remez et al., 2010; Remez et al., 2008). This places great demands on the auditory system and even exceeds the system's basic capabilities (Repp, 1988). As opposed to written language, speech has no blank spaces between words and no commas or full stops. Through multiple steps at timescales of tens to hundreds of milliseconds, the auditory system must transform this signal into phonetic representations that are interpretable to linguistic interfaces in our brains (Chomsky & Halle, 1968), segment the unbroken stream into possible words, make contact with long-term memory storage and finally reach the intended word and achieve comprehension. Even then, words themselves are complex, multi-layered and multi-modal entities (Durst-Andersen & Bentsen, 2021; Elman, 2004, 2009), and we add new words to our lexicon almost every day (Brysbaert et al., 2016). Complicating matters even further, speech is built up of potentially meaningless units – phonemes – that can be combined in countless ways to create and distinguish meaningful morphemes and words (Hjelmslev, 1961 [1943]; Hockett, 1958; Martinet, 1949), and we can even use these to create words or sentences that may never have been heard before but can be understood or guessed by listeners if they are constructed according to the morphosyntax or grammar of a certain language (Chomsky, 1957). As a whole, speech can be considered a code that needs to be cracked by the listener to arrive at the message intended by the speaker (Liberman et al., 1967).

When listening to speech, our brains must map the continuous acoustic signal onto linguistic categories, interface with some type of mental lexicon in long-term memory and recognise the spoken word. There is also always a balance between the speaker's articulatory economy and constraints, and the listener's need for perceptual distinctiveness (Lindblom, 1990). Rather than a set of unique acoustic features neatly corresponding to each possible speech sound in a particular language, there is a *many-to-one* mapping problem inherent to speech that the system needs to overcome. Different speakers produce different speech sounds when pronouncing the same words. They may reduce or drop speech sounds altogether, and one speaker may even pronounce the same speech sounds differently on different occasions (Allen, Miller, & DeSteno, 2003; R. S. Newman, Clouse, & Burnham, 2001). Similar or identical speech sounds may also lead to different word meanings depending on their context in a word. The *s* in the word *skit* contributes differently to its meaning than the *s* in *kits*. In English, the presence or lack of a puff of aspiration after the initial plosive phoneme /k/ of the word *cat* does not change its meaning: it is merely treated as variance in the signal that still leads – through the transformation from signal to phonetic representations and categories – to the 'invariant' perception of the English phoneme /k/, regardless of its allophonic manifestation. In a language like Hindi, however, where aspiration is phonemic, such a sound difference can change the meanings of words, so that aspirated and unaspirated instances of /k/ in the speech stream need to be mapped to two different phonemes.

This is an overview of the challenges faced and – seemingly easily – overcome by the neural auditory system as it processes speech. Beginning with the history of neurolinguistics from the nineteenth century to the present day, it discusses modern neuroimaging methods and analysis techniques before a description of sound and speech, and how they are processed by the brain from cochlea to cortex, finishing with a few directions in which the field of phonetics in the brain is moving into the future.

2 The Birth of Neurolinguistics

2.1 Paul Broca: The Seat of Language

The foundations of cognitive neuroscience, neuropsychology and the subsequent development of neurolinguistics – as well as attendant neuro-prefixed subdisciplines such as neurophonetics – were arguably laid in the 1860s through the work of Paul Broca (1824–1880), a surgeon and anatomist based in Paris who studied the connection between brain damage and function. At the time, there were ongoing discussions about the localisation of brain functions, including the seat of language functions in the brain. The idea that brain functions could be localised to restricted areas of the cerebral cortex – the outermost layer of the brain, folded into grooves (*sulci*, singular *sulcus*) and ridges (*gyri*, singular *gyrus*) – had been contested but gained popularity through the work of Franz Gall and colleagues (Gall & Spurzheim, 1809). However, Gall viewed brain function through the framework of phrenology: the idea that the localisation of brain functions could be ascertained through measurements of bumps on the skull. While Paul Broca's subsequent research into the connection between brain injury and language function would serve to discredit the claims of the phrenologists by showing that distinct areas of the brain were, in fact, important for language function, he was not the first to suggest a connection between pathology and brain function. A few decades earlier, Jean-Baptiste Bouillaud (1825) presented several cases of patients who had lost the ability to speak but could still understand spoken language. While their damage was too extensive to draw any conclusions as to localised lesions, Bouillaud suggested that the anterior – or frontal – lobes contain an *organe législateur de la parole*: the legislative organ of speech, which could be paralysed in the absence of any other paralysis, and which contained subsystems for both the 'intellectual' (in the grey matter, i.e., neuronal cell bodies) and 'muscular' facets of speech (white matter, i.e., connections between cells). As we will see, the frontal lobes of the brain indeed contain crucial centres for speech and language – one named after Paul Broca himself – but the particular importance of the *left* hemisphere for language did not reach the mainstream until the Paris anatomist published his findings in the 1860s, with a previous similar suggestion by neurologist Marc Dax in 1836 having gone largely unnoticed (Dax, 1865).

On 11 April 1861, 51-year-old Louis Leborgne was admitted to Bicêtre hospital in Paris under the care of Paul Broca. Leborgne's only response to questions was the syllable 'tan' repeated twice, accompanied by left-hand gestures (Broca, 1861b, 1861c). The speed at which he had lost his ability to speak was unknown, but when he was admitted to hospital, he had not spoken for two or three months. While he understood everything said to him and appeared to have good hearing, all he could say in return was 'tan tan'. Broca suggested that the lesion had been relatively limited in size for the first ten years, but subsequently led to increasing paralysis of the limbs. The goal was now to identify the primary location of this lesion, and the suggestion was that it started in the left frontal lobe and spread to left subcortical areas. Twenty-four hours after Leborgne's death on 17 April, an autopsy was conducted. It was concluded that the most extensive substance loss had occurred in the posterior part of the left inferior frontal gyrus, and that the lesion must have begun to form there, causing the aphemia – defined as damage to the faculty responsible for articulating words, a condition subsequently known as *(motor) aphasia* – and then slowly over the course of ten years spread to the insula as well as subcortical areas, leading to limb paralysis. Broca saw this connection between the brain damage and loss of speech as evidence that the localisation of the 'seat' of spoken language is incompatible with *le système des bosses* – phrenology – which had previously been proposed by Franz Gall. This general language faculty was proposed to establish connections between ideas and signs – foreshadowing the theoretical work of Ferdinand De Saussure (1916) – and like Bouillaud before him, Broca made a distinction between the production and perception of language, the former but not the latter being damaged in the case of Leborgne.

Later that year, another patient – eighty-four-year-old Lazare Lelong – was admitted to Bicêtre for femoral surgery (Broca, 1861a). Following a fall and brain haemorrhage a year and a half earlier, he could only speak a few words, with difficulty, while he still understood everything that was said to him. The words he could produce did carry meaning in French: *oui* ('yes'), *non* ('no'), *tois [trois]* ('three'), *toujours* ('always') and *Lelo* for Lelong. *Trois* appeared to encompass all numbers (he would say *trois* and indicate he meant 'four' with his fingers: the number of children he had), and *toujours* did not seem to have any specific meaning. Again, Broca concluded that what had been lost was the 'faculty of articulated speech' (*faculté du langage articulé*), but it was different from Leborgne, in that the patient could say several words and thus had a limited 'vocabulary'. Lelong passed away on 8 November 1861. Following an autopsy, a lesion was found in the left frontal lobe. While it was considerably less widely spread than Leborgne's lesion, it was noted that the 'centre' of Lelong's lesion was in the same spot as the former: the posterior part of the left inferior frontal gyrus. Pars opercularis and pars triangularis of the inferior frontal gyrus are today commonly referred to as *Broca's area* (Brodmann, 1909). While the lesions present in these patients were subsequently found to extend more than Broca initially assumed (Dronkers et al., 2007) – in fact, Broca's aphasia is commonly associated with damage to areas outside this area (Mohr et al., 1978) – we now know that Broca's area indeed plays important roles in the articulation of speech as well as in semantic and syntactic processing (Goucha & Friederici, 2015).

Broca summarised his ideas about the lateralisation of language function by claiming that 'we speak with the left hemisphere', but that there is a minority of people who process speech in the right hemisphere. He was careful to note, however, that even in 'left-brained' people, the left hemisphere was not the only possible seat of the language faculty, that is, where the link between ideas and linguistic signs is established. Since the link between these concepts appeared intact in those patients who were still able to perceive and meaningfully comprehend language, Broca hinted that the general language faculty may be spread out over more areas, but gave only the broad suggestion that the right hemisphere of the brain may take on this role in case of damage to the left hemisphere (Broca, 1865).

2.2 Carl Wernicke: From Production to Perception

In the next decade, the discussion of language function and pathology in the brain expanded from language production to include the perception of speech.

Another important innovation was the beginning of a move from isolated 'seats' of functions in the brain to recognising the importance of associations, or connections, between areas. German anatomist and neuropathologist Carl Wernicke (1848–1905) was inspired by Theodor Meynert, with whom he studied for six months, as well as by the work of Paul Broca. Meynert was a proponent of models of brain function that not only included discrete localised areas but also the connections between them, and – like Broca – he had also investigated the connection between aphasia and brain injury (Whitaker & Etlinger, 1993). Wernicke's *Der aphasische Symptomenkomplex* [The Aphasic Syndrome] (1874) references Meynert's ideas and was based on descriptions of patients who appeared to mainly have deficits in comprehending rather than producing speech. The first such description concerned a fifty-nine-year-old woman presenting with nausea and headaches. She could use words and phrases correctly and spontaneously but could only understand a few spoken words, with great difficulty. The second – a woman of seventy-five years who was initially assumed to be deaf – could not answer any questions correctly and used only a small number of words in her confused and garbled speech. Wernicke concluded that these patients had lost their ability to understand spoken language and that they showed signs of *sensory* or receptive aphasia. This contrasted with Broca's patients, whose aphasia was primarily *expressive*. Wernicke suggested that the symptoms of sensory aphasia in these patients were due to damage to a posterior part of the left superior temporal gyrus (STG), which we commonly refer to today as part of *Wernicke's area*. However, it is important to note that definitions of the actual area – as is also the case with Broca's area – often refer to anatomy rather than function (Binder, 2015). Thus, the picture becomes more complex when one considers the myriad functions served by the different constituent parts and cellular composition that make up the 'classical' language areas.

Wernicke applied Meynert's ideas of neural connectivity to begin building an extended model of neurolinguistic brain function. He defined a speech centre where the inferior frontal gyrus – Broca's area – was responsible for motor-articulatory function and Wernicke's area a sensory centre for conceptual 'sound-images' (*Klangbilder*). Wernicke also hypothesised a connection between the sound-image and motor areas. While the sound-image centres were assumed to be distributed bilaterally (across both hemispheres of the brain), the sound-image centre was only connected to the motor centre on the left side of the brain, leading to a generally left-dominant STG. Higher cognitive functions of the brain were thus not assumed to be localised to particular areas but arose as a result of connections between cortical areas. Wernicke originally proposed that the pathway between these two language centres would run through the insula, but later accepted that the relevant structure is the *arcuate fasciculus*, a bundle of fibres that connects temporal and parietal areas with the frontal lobe (Dejerine, 1895; Geschwind, 1967). Wernicke even hypothesised that damage to this connection would give rise to a new type of aphasia – *Leitungsaphasie*, or conduction aphasia – and he correctly predicted that this type of aphasia would lead to problems with spoken word or sentence repetition. Even though conduction aphasia is now known to be associated with damage to areas in the temporal and parietal cortices rather than the arcuate fasciculus (Buchsbaum et al., 2011; Shuren et al., 1995), this prediction was a testament to the innovation and explanatory power of his model.

2.3 From Neuroanatomy to Neuropsychology and Cognitive Neuroscience

Wernicke's model was subsequently updated by German physician Ludwig Lichtheim (1885), whose aim was to describe the pathways necessary for both normal language function and pathology, and to relate functions to neuro-physiology. He achieved this by adding complexities and nodes to Wernicke's more rudimentary diagrams (see Figure 1), suggesting that once normal language function is established through the diagram and its assumed neurophysio-logical underpinnings, it would be possible to define language disorders by assuming lesions along the pathways. In this way, Broca's aphasia was caused by damage to the 'motor centre of speech' (area M), Wernicke's a result of damage to area A (the acoustic word-centre), conduction aphasia as a result of damage to the connection between M and A, and so on. It was also assumed that

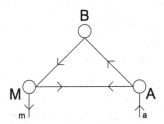

Figure 1 Simplified diagram showing the main connections for speech perception and production in the Wernicke-Lichtheim model (adapted from Lichtheim (1885)). The connection *m* shows the articulatory 'muscle' (speech production) pathway between the brainstem and area *M* (the motor centre of speech, corresponding to Broca's area), while *a* signifies the pathway between the auditory brainstem and *A* (the acoustic word-centre, corresponding to Wernicke's area). Node *B* signifies semantic concepts distributed across the brain.

node B, responsible for the elaboration of (semantic) concepts in accordance with Wernicke and connected to both A and M, was distributed over many areas of the cortex, something which has since been corroborated using modern neuroimaging techniques (Huth et al., 2016). Damage to the pathway B-M was associated with a condition today known as transcortical motor aphasia, linked to areas surrounding Broca's area. The symptoms of this disorder are similar to those of Broca's aphasia, with the main difference being that patients with transcortical motor aphasia can repeat words and sentences (Berthier et al., 1991).

The Wernicke-Lichtheim model and its focus on tying together models of brain function with underlying physiology constituted a crucial milestone for the development of modern neuropsychology and cognitive neuroscience. Another important contribution was the detailed map of the cerebral cortex by German neurologist Korbinian Brodmann (1909). Brodmann identified fifty-two regions of the cortex based on their cytoarchitectonic features, that is, their cellular composition. His map is still extensively used to refer to cortical areas today, with the abbreviation BA for 'Brodmann area'. For example, Broca's area is commonly defined as being made up of pars opercularis, or BA44, and pars triangularis, or BA45, two areas that Brodmann identified as being closely cytoarchitectonically related, while Wernicke's area is often associated with BA22, the posterior part of the superior temporal gyrus, and BA40, the supra-marginal gyrus, which borders BA22 with no sharp cytoarchitectonic boundary.

In the 1960s, American neurologist Norman Geschwind published highly influential papers that drew on and further updated the connectionist model of brain function (Geschwind, 1965a, 1965b). He stressed the importance of understanding disorders like aphasia as disorders of disconnections of either white matter pathways between primary receptive and motor areas or parts of the cortex known as association areas ('obligatory way stations'), which receive inputs from multiple areas of the brain. Moreover, Geschwind extended the area of research from patient case studies to the mammalian brain in humans and other animals. In particular, he suggested that the inferior parietal lobule – comprising the angular and supramarginal gyri – is unique to humans among the primates due to its importance for speech processing. This evolutionarily advanced association area is surrounded by other association areas, leading Geschwind to call it the 'association area of association areas', or a secondary association area. It is involved in forming the cross-modal associations between auditory and visual representations and thus plays a role in language-specific tasks such as object naming and semantic processing (see Section 5). However, it also underpins more domain-general complex cognitive functions, such as future planning, spatial attention and social cognition (Numssen, Bzdok, & Hartwigsen, 2021).

The second half of the twentieth century saw rapid and paradigm-shifting advances in both linguistic theory (Chomsky, 1965a, 1965b) and cognitive neuroscience and methodology, as well as the establishment and development of psycholinguistics throughout the century as a fruitful and innovative field of research (Cutler, 2012). With these advances, the speech and language models of Broca and Wernicke turned out to be both anatomically and linguistically underspecified (Poeppel & Hickok, 2004). It has become clear that language comprises a number of complex systems – phonology, phonetics, syntax, semantics and so on, each made up of separate subsystems and each overlapping with other systems – and that neurolinguistic theories of brain function have to take into account the fact that language processing capacities underpinning these systems appear to be distributed across the brain: both hemispheres of the brain are involved, and processing takes place in both cortical and subcortical structures. To understand how language is processed in the brain, we need detailed theories of how both language and the brain work, with both sets of theories informing and constraining each other to create linking hypotheses and testable predictions.

Based on these theoretical and methodological advances from the decades leading into the twenty-first century, Hickok and Poeppel (2000, 2004) presented a functional anatomical framework of the cortical organisation of speech perception, as well as an account of different types of aphasias. It was grounded in the nineteenth century idea that speech processing and comprehension necessarily involve interfaces with a conceptual and a motor-articulatory system. The framework drew inspiration from previous work on cortical vision and auditory processing that had identified functionally and anatomically differentiated processing streams in the cerebral cortex (Milner & Goodale, 1995; Rauschecker, 1998; Ungerleider & Mishkin, 1982): a *ventral* and a *dorsal* stream (Latin *venter*, 'belly'; *dorsum,* 'back [of the body]'). Since all tasks involving speech appear to activate the STG, the early first stages of speech perception are proposed to involve auditory-responsive cortical fields in the STG bilaterally, that is, on both the left and right sides of the brain, albeit with some functional asymmetry, as originally suggested by Wernicke. This asymmetric lateralisation means that sound is processed differentially by the two hemispheres. For example, it has been suggested that the left hemisphere specialises in temporal processing and the right specialises in analysing spectral information (Zatorre, 1997). Alternatively, the left hemisphere may specialise in shorter temporal integration windows – faster sample rates (25–50 ms) – while the right specialises in longer windows, or slower sampling rates

(150–250 ms) (Poeppel, 2001, 2003). Yet another reason for the left-hemisphere dominance for speech sounds is that categorical perception – a crucial speech perception mechanism (see Section 4) – appears to be subserved by areas in the left temporal lobe (Liebenthal et al., 2005).

After the acoustic-phonetic analysis, processing is split into two streams. The dorsal stream is critical for mapping sound onto auditory-motor (articulatory) representations, while the ventral stream maps sound onto meaning. The processing streams are bidirectional, so that they underpin both speech perception and production. Thus, the dorsal stream is involved in verbatim repetition tasks that require a mapping from conceptual to articulatory motor representations, and it may play a role in but is not critical for speech perception in passive listening conditions. The ventral stream is broadly responsible for comprehension, that is, the conversion of continuous speech input to something that can be analysed linguistically, as well as acoustic-phonetic processing and the interfaces between lexical and morphological and syntactic processing.

3 Neuroimaging

A range of powerful psycholinguistic behavioural paradigms have been devised to infer the structure, flow and time course of information processing in the brain. Examples include speech shadowing, where listeners can repeat incoming speech at latencies of 150–200 ms (Chistovich, 1960); dichotic listening, which can be used to determine the (most often left-dominant) laterality of speech function in individuals (Broadbent, 1954, 1956); word spotting, aimed at testing the process of speech segmentation (see Section 4) (McQueen, Norris, & Cutler, 1994); gating, where progressively longer portions of words are presented to test the time course of lexical processing (Grosjean, 1980); and lexical decision, where listeners determine whether a word is real or not (D. E. Meyer & Schvaneveldt, 1971; Rubenstein, Garfield, & Millikan, 1970). In addition, a number of neuroimaging techniques were developed in the twentieth century to track brain activity in space and time. In the following sections, the focus lies on electroencephalography, but other widely used neuroimaging techniques are functional magnetic resonance imaging (fMRI), magnetoencephalography (MEG) and functional near-infrared spectroscopy (fNIRS).

3.1 Electroencephalography and Functional Magnetic Resonance Imaging

Electroencephalography (EEG) is a non-invasive method for measuring fluctuations in the naturally occurring electrical activity in the brain – measured in microvolts – at the millisecond scale, using electrodes placed on the scalp.

The trace of voltage over time is referred to as the *electroencephalogram*. This electrical activity has its source in brain cells – *neurons* – and can be measured on the scalp. Originating near the cell body of a neuron, *action potentials* are electrical signals that the brain uses to convey, receive, and analyse information. Neurons receive information through several short processes known as *dendrites* and send signals to other neurons through an *axon*, which is a single, tubular process covered in the lipid substance *myelin*. The insulating fatty myelin sheath acts as an insulating layer that increases the speed of action potentials. The axon ends in *synapses,* which contact other neurons. A transmitting cell is referred to as *presynaptic* and a receiving cell as *postsynaptic*. The activity reflected in the electroencephalogram is overwhelmingly made up of summed postsynaptic potentials (about 10–100 ms) as a result of activity in large groups of similarly oriented neurons rather than individual action potentials (about 1 ms), with the exception of the early auditory brainstem response (ABR), which reflects action potentials generated in the cochlea that travel through the auditory nerve (Pratt, 2011). Thus, the functional temporal resolution of EEG is commonly between tens and hundreds rather than single milliseconds.

The temporal resolution of EEG is in contrast with *functional magnetic resonance imaging* which measures the comparatively slower magnetic signatures of blood flow to areas in the brain active in response to certain conditions (Ogawa et al., 1990). Put simply, as an area becomes active – compared to a baseline of, for example, rest or silence – blood flows to the area with every heartbeat to provide it with oxygen, replace the deoxygenated blood and replenish energy. In fact, more oxygen than is needed according to neuronal energy consumption is delivered to areas with increased neural activation (Fox et al., 1988). The main dependent variable in fMRI analyses – *blood-oxygen-level-dependent signal* (BOLD) – is not a result of an increase in deoxygenated blood in active areas (which actually decreases the BOLD signal (Ogawa & Lee, 1990; Ogawa et al., 1990)), but rather due to oxygenated blood washing the deoxygenated blood away, providing an indirect but highly useful link between neural activity and the fMRI signal. It takes several seconds for oxygenated blood to saturate an area. Thus, the temporal resolution of fMRI and the BOLD signal is orders of magnitude slower than that of EEG (seconds vs. milliseconds). However, the spatial resolution of fMRI is excellent, allowing researchers to track active brain areas and networks at the scale of millimetres and below in three dimensions across the entire brain, including subcortical areas and areas deep within the brain. As such, it is mainly used to answer questions of 'where' something happens in the brain rather than 'when', including at the level of separate cortical layers (Lawrence et al., 2019). Both neuroimaging methods can be combined and used concurrently with specialised EEG equipment and pre-processing methods, enabling correlations between BOLD signal and EEG amplitude to answer research questions that require both spatial and temporal data.

A technique which is closely related to EEG – magnetoencephalography – has been used to illustrate the time course of information transmission between different areas in the brain, taking full advantage of the excellent temporal resolution and the additional spatial resolution offered by the electromagnetic properties of groups of neurons as measured using MEG (Pulvermüller & Shtyrov, 2008; Pulvermüller, Shtyrov, & Ilmoniemi, 2003).

3.2 EEG and Event-Related Potentials

By placing electrodes on the scalp (normally ranging from 32 to 128, and up to 256 electrodes) and amplifying the signal, the voltage at each electrode can be tracked over time relative to a reference electrode placed away from the scalp. The reference electrode is ideally placed in a location where it picks up as little neural activity as possible, commonly the mastoid process behind the ear. The average signal of all electrodes can also serve as a reference. However, there is no perfect reference, and it should be chosen carefully since it can influence the data significantly. The temporal resolution of the signal depends on the sampling rate used for the recording, such that a 1 kHz rate provides a voltage reading per electrode every millisecond, 250 Hz every four milliseconds and so on. The highest measurable frequency depends on the sampling rate so that the highest frequency that can be resolved is half the sampling rate (the *Nyquist theorem*). With a 250 Hz sampling rate, the highest reliably resolvable frequency is 125 Hz, or the *Nyquist frequency*. In addition to this, filters are usually applied to the EEG so that frequencies above and below certain thresholds are attenuated, and noise can be suppressed. High-pass filters – attenuating low frequencies – can help suppress slow drifts in the signal, often caused by perspiration (Picton & Hillyard, 1972). Low-pass filters, which attenuate frequencies above a certain threshold, have an anti-aliasing effect (attenuating potentially artifactual frequencies greater than the Nyquist frequency) and they also act to reduce the effect of high-frequency electromyographic muscle artifacts. The bone and connective tissue surrounding the brain act as a natural low-pass filter of frequencies, but also as a spatial filter, so that the signal is smeared and spread out against the skull (Srinivasan et al., 1996). Thus, while EEG has excellent temporal resolution at the millisecond scale, its spatial resolution is poor: there is an infinite number of possible neural generators that can explain any given data measured on the scalp (the *inverse problem*).

The raw output of an EEG recording contains contributions from many different sources, such as muscle or cardiac activity, body movements and mains electricity noise, many of which have a signal strength orders of magnitude stronger than those of neural signals. There are various methods for reducing the impact of noise and artifacts. For example, discrete artifacts such as eye-blinks can be attenuated and effectively removed (Jung et al., 2000), and this is commonly combined with amplitude cut-offs so that trials with amplitude fluctuations of ±100 µV are discarded before the final averaging and analysis, though some have argued for minimal pre-processing of relatively clean EEG data obtained in laboratory conditions (Delorme, 2023). By averaging the EEG, neural responses to events – such as a visually or auditorily presented stimulus – can be isolated from the noise, leading to the extraction of *event-related potentials* (ERPs). These waveforms are time-locked to events and consist of negative or positive voltage deflections relative to a baseline, referred to as *peaks* or *components*, which can be defined as changes in voltage that vary systematically across conditions and subjects (Luck, 2014). Some components, such as P1, N1 and P2, are named based on whether the deflection is positive ('P') or negative ('N') relative to the baseline, as well as their occurrence relative to other waveforms (so that P2 is the second positive deflection after P1). These particular components – the P1-N1-P2 complex – are obligatorily evoked by auditory stimuli (Näätänen & Picton, 1987), such as pure tones or spoken words, and reflect the detection of auditory onsets as well as their acoustic properties. Other components may have more descriptive names, such as the mismatch negativity (MMN), a widely used component that appears in response to a stimulus that deviates from previously repeated stimuli, indicating that the participant has perceived the difference between the two types of stimuli (Näätänen, Gaillard, & Mäntysalo, 1978). There are a number of more or less descriptively named components that are useful for speech research. The *phonological mismatch* (or *mapping*) *negativity* (PMN) is elicited by mismatched phonemes in words otherwise expected based on the sentence context (Connolly & Phillips, 1994; R. L. Newman & Connolly, 2009; R. L. Newman et al., 2003) and the *left-anterior negativity* (LAN) – named after its usual topographical distribution on the scalp – is found for morphosyntactic violations (A. J. Newman et al., 2007; Osterhout & Mobley, 1995).

When the EEG is averaged into event-related potentials, an ERP is obtained for each condition and each electrode site, in time-windows or *epochs* ranging from hundreds to thousands of milliseconds, and a baseline window of 100–200 ms. The most common analysis is of signal *amplitude* in a time-window, and this measurement is relative to the baseline. Thus, the experimenter must take care to ensure that the baseline does not differ between conditions since this may introduce confounds and influence the interpretation of ERPs. For example, if there is consistent noise in baselines in condition A but not in condition B, or if condition A stimuli are preceded by silence and stimuli in B are not, this will be reflected in the ERPs.

ERPs are by definition tied to events, the onset of which may be more or less difficult to define. The onset of an auditory stimulus from silence constitutes a relatively well-defined context from which to time-lock and extract an ERP. However, this may be difficult to obtain in studies of intonation or other prosodic phenomena, for example, where the definition of a discrete, perceptually relevant event for time-locking could be more elusive, leading to temporal jitter that could mask small or short-lasting effects in the data. In these cases, it is important to perform detailed acoustic analyses of the stimuli to ascertain that event onsets are well controlled and that the baseline does not vary between conditions.

Since an ERP is obtained for each electrode site, one can calculate *difference waves* – reflecting the total amplitude difference over time between conditions A and B in a certain time-window – and subsequently construct a scalp map or *topography* of a component, showing its distribution across the scalp. In the case of the mismatch negativity, for example, the specific topography may vary depending on stimulus features, but it typically displays a frontal distribution (Alho, 1995), skewed towards the right hemisphere, except for language-related deviants which tend to show left-lateralised MMNs (Tervaniemi & Hugdahl, 2003). Component scalp topography is further influenced by the choice of reference site, and this must be taken into consideration when inspecting topography plots. While it is essentially impossible to infer the source of brain activity from component topography, it can be a useful tool to argue in favour of – or rule out – interpretations of ERP effects. Thus, if component A reliably shows frontal distributions in the literature and component B is typically posterior, this may be used to interrogate the interpretation of an effect elicited in a carefully controlled experiment.

The temporal resolution of EEG makes it an excellent method for answering a multitude of questions regarding cognitive processes. Like fMRI and other neuroimaging techniques, it does not require an overt response from participants, which means that brain activity can be probed without particular tasks, and the pool of participants that can be tested is expanded to non-verbal or pre-verbal populations, or to participants who cannot physically give overt responses to stimuli. EEG has been referred to as 'reaction time for the 21st century' (Luck, Woodman, & Vogel, 2000). As such, it can provide information about cognitive processes that are more or less invisible to mental chronometry, which may occur after or even before the onset of a stimulus. For example, EEG can reveal subconscious brain responses to phonetic differences between such things as minimally different speech sounds (for example, using the MMN). It can also measure grammaticality or acceptability of linguistic structures, at multiple levels and at the millisecond scale, without overt responses. In addition to this, it allows researchers to ask questions regarding the *ordering and timing* of cognitive processes. Thus, five-month-old pre-verbal infants have been shown to recode complex input into abstract categories within minutes of training, as evidenced by EEG mismatch responses (Kabdebon & Dehaene-Lambertz, 2019). EEG has also been used to show that the brain can tell the difference between real and pseudowords within thirty milliseconds of a mismatching phoneme (Shtyrov & Lenzen, 2017). With regard to the ordering of processes – and a caveat that the underpinnings and drivers of most ERP components still remain to be fully elucidated – two commonly studied ERP components, the N400 and the P600, are often found in succession. This has sparked debates, for example, about whether semantic processing precedes syntactic processing in speech comprehension (Bornkessel-Schlesewsky & Schlesewsky, 2008), or vice versa (Friederici (2002), but see also Steinhauer and Drury (2012) for a critical review. Broadly speaking, the N400 is the default neural response to the semantic content of any potentially meaningful stimulus, occurring at 300–500 milliseconds after its onset. In addition to being modulated by lexical characteristics of words presented in isolation, the N400 amplitude is sensitive to the probability of encountering a word's semantic features given the preceding context, and is larger in cases where a word is semantically unexpected, such as the sentence *He spread the warm bread with socks* (Kutas & Federmeier, 2011; Kutas & Hillyard, 1980; Kuperberg, Brothers, & Wlotko, 2020; Nour Eddine, Brothers, & Kuperberg, 2022). The P600 occurs at 600–1,000 milliseconds following the onset of a violation (Osterhout & Holcomb, 1992), and is suggested to reflect an error signal and subsequent reprocessing, reanalysis or reinterpretation as the brain tries to determine whether an initial decision was correct. The P600 is not restricted to syntax as previously believed (Brouwer et al., 2017; Knoeferle et al., 2008; Kuperberg et al., 2020), but also appears in response to semantic or thematic incongruities such as *For breakfast, the eggs would only eat …* (Kuperberg et al., 2003), and its function has been connected to another common, non-linguistic neural error signal, the P300 (Coulson, King, & Kutas, 1998; Kuperberg et al., 2020; Sassenhagen, Schlesewsky, & Bornkessel-Schlesewsky, 2014).

In summary, the event-related potential technique allows researchers to gain insight into both the actual phenomena of written and spoken language, as well as the neural mechanisms that give rise to these potentials on the scalp.

The latter can be achieved by combining EEG with fMRI to investigate the neural source of ERP components, or by computational modelling, where researchers build algorithmic models to determine which factors are necessary to give rise to effects similar to those found in ERPs. This is then used to create new hypotheses and predictions for further study. Much knowledge of ERPs has also come from meticulous and replicated experimental work. Alternatively, ERPs can be and are often used as an experimental tool without necessarily referencing the underlying mechanisms. For example, to determine whether native or second-language speakers can tell the difference between speech sound categories, such as dental and retroflex plosives, the presence of an MMN indicates that they are indeed perceived as different sounds. The MMN is also useful since it persists even in the absence of attention: participants often watch a silent film to divert attention to the stimuli, but the MMN still occurs to signal perceptual differences between standard and deviant stimuli. Finding a LAN would, for example, suggest a subject-verb number agreement error (Osterhout & Mobley, 1995). Language learning has been tested using a methodology based on the N400 and P600 components: early learners have been shown to display an N400-like effect to syntactic errors, which changes to a P600 for later, more advanced learners (Osterhout et al., 2008).

3.3 Statistical Analysis of EEG Data

Traditionally, the amplitudes of event-related potentials have been interrogated using analyses of variance (ANOVAs). The experimenter chooses a time-window in which to extract average ERP amplitudes from the experimental conditions (the dependent variable) and performs an analysis which can include both within-subject (in an MMN experiment, this might be an experimental contrast between two phonemes of interest to the experimenter: one as a standard and one as a deviant) and between-subject factors (such as native/non-native speakers). Thus, data is averaged over time-windows, conditions and participants, and entered into a repeated-measures ANOVA. For the mismatch negativity, the dependent variable is often the difference between the average response to the standard stimulus and the average deviant response, that is, a difference wave. The MMN typically peaks between 100–250 ms (Näätänen, 1995; Schröger, 1997), and this is consequently a common à priori time-window for the statistical analysis of this component. Additionally, topographical factors are included in the ANOVA. This commonly involves a factor covering clusters of electrode sites along the anterior-central-posterior axis of the scalp as well as a laterality factor (left-right or left-midline-right). Interrogating interactions between these factors could thus reveal differences between experimental conditions with – for example – left-anterior or right-posterior topographical distributions, and so on.

A common issue that arises in EEG data analysis is that pre-processing steps such as artifact rejection may lead to missing data, so that the number of observations differs across conditions, violating core equal-variance assumptions used in ANOVAs. One proposed solution is mixed-effects models (Baayen, Davidson, & Bates, 2008), which are more robust in this respect and decrease the risk of Type I errors, that is, rejecting the null hypothesis when it is actually true (false positive). Furthermore, mixed-effects models have the advantage of allowing the experimenter to account for the effect of participant and item variability (Barr et al., 2013) – *random effects* – on the dependent variable, as well as include both categorical and continuous variables in the analysis of EEG data (N. J. Smith & Kutas, 2015).

Neuroimaging data is also highly multidimensional, with potentially thousands of readings per second (time) per electrode site (space) in an EEG recording. What is often referred to as the *multiple-comparisons problem* arises from the large number of simultaneous statistical comparisons, which increases the risk of erroneous statistical inferences such as Type I (false positive) and II (false negative) errors. The problem can be exacerbated by the experimenter visually inspecting the waveforms to choose a time-window (or cluster of electrodes) for analysis where the difference between conditions appears largest but may simply be due to noise. It is therefore recommended that researchers select time-windows and electrode sites for analysis in a theory-driven manner, based on à priori assumptions from the literature (such as in the MMN example in Section 3.2). Another data-driven way of analysing ERPs and correcting for multiple comparisons is the non-parametric cluster-based permutation approach, which has gained popularity in recent years. Here, *data-driven* refers to the fact that – apart from extracting epochs time-locked to events – one does not need to know the spatiotemporal distribution of the effect in advance: it allows for 'prior ignorance', as well as exploratory analyses of potentially novel phenomena (Maris & Oostenveld, 2007; Sassenhagen & Draschkow, 2019). This method does not require the researcher to select a particular time-window for analysis, and it solves the multiple-comparisons problem by reducing comparisons of condition differences in each sample to a single comparison between experimental conditions in a spatiotemporal grid (Maris & Oostenveld, 2007), thereby decreasing type I error rates (Pernet et al., 2015). It also takes advantage of the fact that in high-dimensional spatiotemporal data such as EEG, clusters of adjacent electrodes (and time-points) are likely to show similar effects in time and space, leading to increased statistical sensitivity – and a lower type II error rate – compared to methods such as Bonferroni correction, by providing prior knowledge about the expected effect (Maris & Oostenveld, 2007). However, while cluster-based permutation techniques have been claimed and used to find the time at which effects begin (effect onset) in the literature, this type of analysis does not in fact test the statistical significance of effect latency (i.e., its onset in milliseconds) or topography (scalp distribution). Thus, care must be taken when interpreting the analysis output, so as not to overstate the significance of latency or topography results (Sassenhagen & Draschkow, 2019).

Yet another increasingly popular method for analysing EEG data is *multivariate pattern analysis* (MVPA). MVPA encompasses a set of neuroimaging analysis methods where machine-learning classifier algorithms use patterns of brain activation to 'decode' the underlying model that explains the data. A subset of the neuroimaging data is used to train the classifier to distinguish a reliable difference in brain activation pattern between the experimental conditions, which can be tested using parametric tests such as Student's *t*-test or nonparametric tests like the Wilcoxon signed-rank test or permutation tests, with different options for addressing the multiple-comparisons problem (Grootswagers, Wardle, & Carlson, 2017). The classifier's decoding accuracy can be tracked over time at the millisecond scale, making MVPA an excellent tool to investigate the temporal dynamics of neural processes and information processing in the brain. As in traditional ERP analyses, the data can consist of evoked brain responses to stimuli, such as images or sounds. Like cluster-based permutation, MVPA allows for similar 'prior ignorance', as well as exploratory analyses, regarding the spatial distribution and timing of effects. It can also have increased sensitivity compared to traditional univariate approaches, with multivariate techniques more capable of detecting subtle differences between conditions at an earlier stage (Cauchoix et al., 2014). A typical use of MVPA decoding could be an experiment where a participant views green squares or blue circles, while their brain activity is recorded using EEG or MEG. The aim is then to predict – based on patterns of brain activation – whether the participant viewed a green square or a blue circle, with the assumption that the brain activation patterns differ between the two conditions (Grootswagers et al., 2017). In spoken-language research, MVPA has been used to investigate multiple levels of linguistic processing simultaneously, tracking near-parallel brain responses to grammatical and ungrammatical structures, words and pseudowords, as well as semantic features in task-free paradigms, allowing the inclusion of participants unable to give an overt response, such as those with brain damage or children with developmental disorders (Jensen, Hyder, & Shtyrov, 2019). At lower levels of speech perception, MVPA has begun to be used to investigate long-standing questions, taking advantage of its excellent tracking of temporal dynamics in information processing. Beach et al. (2021) applied MVPA to MEG brain responses to syllables on the *ba-da* continuum in active and passive listening conditions to investigate the stages involved in the transformation from detailed (continuous) acoustic analysis to (categorical) phonemic representations, to determine for how long subphonemic information is available. Stimulus decoding accuracy above chance began at 165 milliseconds, underpinned chiefly by activity in the left hemisphere. It was observed for longer when a response was required, suggesting that decision-relevant stimulus information was available for longer in the active condition. Furthermore, even when a categorical phoneme representation had been reached (see Section 4), subphonemic information was still available, something which may be important in higher levels of spoken-word recognition and lexical processing, allowing recovery from an initial word interpretation that turns out to be incorrect (McMurray, Tanenhaus, & Aslin, 2009), as well as for perceptual processes such as compensation for coarticulation (see Section 4).

4 From Sound to Perception

Sound is a sensation produced by waves of energy that cause pressure changes in the air. The number of pressure changes – increases and decreases in air pressure – per time period is referred to as the *frequency* of the sound, measured in Hertz (Hz, cycles per second). The size of the wave is referred to as its *amplitude*. The range of hearing for young, healthy adult humans is around 20–20,000 Hz (Fletcher, 1940). Speech is a complex and rapidly changing sound signal, made up of a *spectrum* of sound waves with different frequencies and amplitudes. As a comparison, the *timbre* of an instrument is one of the main distinguishing factors between the sound of an oboe or a bassoon playing the same note at the same volume, where sound waves emanating from these instruments have different spectra – or increased magnitude at certain frequencies – leading, along with some other factors, to the perception of a bassoon or an oboe. The perception of speech sounds is similarly dependent upon changes in the sound spectrum over time. When we listen to speech, peaks or components at certain frequencies in the spectrum can lead to the perception of a certain speech sound, such as a vowel or a consonant. These peaks are commonly referred to as *formants* and are numbered from 1 upwards (F1, F2, F3 and so on). The *fundamental frequency* (F0) underlies the perception of the pitch of the sound, so that a middle C has a fundamental frequency of 512 Hz, and the F0 of A is 440 Hz, with octaves at double those values and harmonics as multiples of the fundamental. Fundamental frequency in speech varies between 100–250 Hz (Peterson & Barney, 1952). However, pitch can still be perceived even if all F0 energy is removed (the *missing fundamental* effect), and thus the perception of pitch is more complex than a simple tracking of the fundamental frequency (Hall & Peters, 1981).

The vocal tract, including constrictions produced by the tongue, teeth and lips, acts as a filter of the signal originating in the glottis, and this leads to formants, or peaks, of acoustic energy in the speech signal at certain frequencies (Fant, 1970). Formants are a result of factors such as the configuration or length of the vocal tract from the glottis to the lips – such that longer vocal tracts lead to lower formant frequencies – as well as parts of the vocal tract modulating the acoustic sound waves along the way. In this way, an important difference between the words *tar* and *tea* in a non-rhotic version of English (where post-vocalic /r/ is absent) lies in the formant structure of the vowels: the height of the tongue body modulates the frequency of the first formant (F1), so that low vowels (as in *tar*) have a higher-frequency F1 than high vowels (*tea*) (Peterson & Barney, 1952). In addition to this, the vowel in *tea* is articulated with the tongue body to the front of the mouth, leading to a higher second formant (F2) than the vowel in *tar*, which is articulated further back in the mouth. In this way, the two-dimensional *vowel space* of a particular language or speaker can be modelled as a function of first and second formant frequency and thus along the low-high and front-back dimensions.

A purely monochromatic – single-wavelength – sinusoidal wave cannot transmit any information, and thus changes or modulations to the carrier signal are crucial for the transmission of information (Picinbono, 1997). From the structures of the ear all the way to the cerebral cortex, the auditory system acts as an analyser of (patterns of) frequency but also of the temporal information of sound, such as changes or modulations in sound amplitude over time, including silences that contain no energy but may be informationally salient with regard to features such as stop consonant voicing (Repp, 1988; Rosen, 1992). All natural sounds involve patterns of amplitude modulation. The auditory system decomposes complex sounds into a number of filtered signals divided into different frequency bands (Fletcher, 1940; Moore, Glasberg, & Baer, 1997), but ultimately accomplishes the subsequent integration of these frequencies to give rise to the percept of speech sounds such as vowels rather than a disjointed collection of formant frequencies (Repp, 1988). All natural sounds such as music and speech can be described in the form of amplitude modulations over time and frequency (Singh & Theunissen, 2003). These modulations are crucial for speech perception (Chi et al., 1999), and the auditory system appears to be highly selective towards and specialised for amplitude-modulated natural sounds such as speech (Joris, Schreiner, & Rees, 2004; Koumura, Terashima, & Furukawa, 2023; Liang, Lu, & Wang, 2002; Yin et al., 2011). The system is also robust to degraded spectral resolution (Remez et al., 1981) – something which often occurs in hearing-impaired listeners or users of cochlear implants – so long as amplitude modulations are preserved. When spectral information is degraded, cues to voicing and manner in consonants are still correctly perceived, whereas the perception of vowels or of consonantal place of articulation – which require more spectral information – is less accurate (Loizou, Dorman, & Tu, 1999; Shannon, Zeng, & Wygonski, 1998; Shannon et al., 1995). An important concept in the neural processing of speech is the *amplitude envelope*, which refers to changes to intensity and duration in sound amplitude – including falls and rises – over time, across a range of frequency bands. A simple fluctuating amplitude envelope can be created by mixing two pure tones with slightly differing frequency, something which will give rise to the perception of beats (Helmholtz, 1877/1895) and is occasionally used by musicians to tune instruments to a reference pitch. Another concept is the *temporal fine structure* of sound. In terms of signal processing, the fine structure can be viewed as a carrier signal, while the envelope is an amplitude modulator of that signal (Hilbert, 1912). A word spoken in isolation will bring about an onset of the amplitude envelope above the ambient noise level of the environment. The rate at which the amplitude rises (its *rise time* from onset to maximum amplitude) is an important cue to things such as speech rhythm. Listeners are also more sensitive to spectro-temporal features of sound onsets than offsets, such that sound onsets receive greater perceptual weighting (Phillips, Hall, & Boehnke, 2002). Fluctuations in factors such as intensity give rise to the perception of loudness, while the duration of modulations can be heard as differences in vowel length, such as English *hit* and *heat*. Conversely, offsets in the envelope can be important cues to segmental information, syllable structure, or the endings of words or phrases. The envelope thus represents relatively slow fluctuations in amplitude over time and can be imagined as the upper and lower outlines of the speech signal. Its different frequency bands contain different information that is useful for perceiving speech, as well as information linked to the physical characteristics of the speaker. Many parallel streams of information thus occur and are processed simultaneously, but across different timescales. For example, some parts of the speech signal, such as prosodic phrase-boundary marking, can occur over longer timescales (several seconds) than others, such as the realisation of stop consonants, which occur over tens of milliseconds. Fast or transient changes in envelope amplitude are thus an important cue for distinguishing consonants (such as stops) from non-consonants, and the amplitude information contained over the tens of milliseconds of consonant release burst further acts as a cue to place of articulation, such as the difference between labial *ba* or velar *ka* (Stevens & Blumstein, 1978). Similarly, the perception of segments differing in manner of articulation – for example, the distinction between the voiceless fricative /ʃ/ and affricate /tʃ/ in *sheep* and *cheap* respectively – rely on factors such as the rise time and overall duration of the frication noise (Howell & Rosen, 1983; Repp et al., 1978).

Figure 2 shows the waveform and spectrogram for the spoken sentence *dunk the stale biscuits into strong drink*. The spectrogram does not represent the

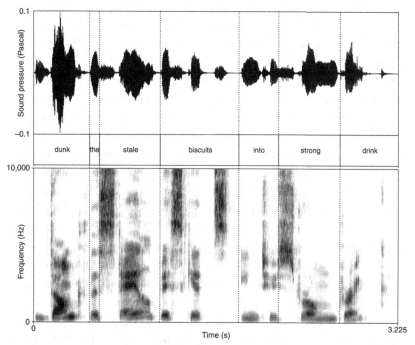

Figure 2 Waveform (top) and spectrogram (bottom) derived using Praat (Boersma & Weenink, 2023) for the sentence *dunk the stale biscuits into strong drink* (IEEE, 1969) spoken by a young adult female speaker of Australian English. The waveform represents envelope amplitude modulations over time, while the spectrogram shows the frequency content of speech over time. Silences are represented as near-zero amplitudes in the waveform and whiter parts, or less energy, in the spectrogram. More energy is shown as darker parts of the spectrogram. Vowels generally have the most energy, as shown by larger amplitudes in the waveform and darker parts of the spectrogram, and vowels occur over longer timescales than the more transient consonants. Note the high frequency content in the sibilants /s/ in *stale, biscuits* and *strong*, exceeding the scale of 10,000 Hz on the *y*-axis. As can be seen in the word *biscuits*, silences – in this case, the plosive occlusion phase before the burst in the stop consonant /k/ – are not necessarily reliable cues to word onsets.

sensory input directly, but rather a transformation of the data which is similar to that undertaken by the auditory system.

Different frequency *bands* of the envelope have been shown to be useful for different types of cues in speech perception, with some bands containing complementary information about similar percepts. Amplitude modulations in the lower frequency band of the envelope (1–50 Hz, or modulations over a range of 20–1,000 ms) contain cues used in the processing of syllables (at around 2–5 Hz, or 200–500 ms). Modulations in this band also provide some information about phonemic segmental identity, such as the difference between voiceless affricates and fricatives. The band between 50 and 500 Hz (2–20 ms) contains information about *periodicity* in the speech signal. For example, the perception of voice pitch or melody is dependent upon changes in fundamental frequency (F0), which in turn is reflective of the rate of change of periodic fluctuations in vocal fold vibrations (Rosen, 1992). An example of a segment marked by increased periodicity or quasi-periodicity is the voiced nasal /m/ in *mat*. Aperiodicity – an irregular or random pattern of fluctuations over time – on the other hand can lead to the perception of noise, voicelessness or frication in segments (such as /h/ in *horse* or /ʃ/ in *ship*) as well as voicing distinctions between allophones. In addition to the concept of lexical competition (Norris, McQueen, & Cutler, 1995), voicing distinctions have been found to be useful in the segmentation of speech. Since spoken language does not include blank spaces between words that are reliable for speech segmentation, we must use other cues to divide or segment the continuous speech signal into discrete items. Thus, the spectral content of the amplitude envelope turns out to be an important perceptual cue to the difference between phrases and words like *night rate* and *nitrate*, where the /r/ is voiced in *night rate* but not in *nitrate*. This is due to the aspiration of the /t/ in *nitrate* rendering the /r/ more aperiodic and thus devoicing it (Lehiste, 1960). While there are no pauses between words in speech, silences between individual speech sounds can, in fact, change phonemic perception. For example, introducing a sufficiently long silent interval between /s/ and /l/ in *slit* can give rise to a percept of *split* (J. Bastian, Eimas, & Liberman, 1961), while an extended silence between the words *grey ship* can result in a percept of *great ship* (Repp et al., 1978). Different languages provide different cues to speech segmentation, involving phonotactics (McQueen, 1998; McQueen & Cox, 1995), vowel phonology (Suomi, McQueen, & Cutler, 1997), metrical structure (Cutler & Norris, 1988; Norris et al., 1995) and lexical prosody (Söderström, Lulaci, & Roll, 2023).

The timbre and formant pattern of the temporal fine structure of sound are contained in the frequency band with a wide range between 600 and 10,000 Hz (Rosen, 1992). The fine structure also carries information important for pitch perception (Z. M. Smith, Delgutte, & Oxenham, 2002). In vowels, high-frequency spectral formant information from vocal tract configuration is crucial for their identity. For example, a vowel articulated to the front of the mouth such as /i/ contains more high-frequency energy than /u/ which is articulated to the back of the mouth. Whereas consonants are marked by rapid spectral changes at around 10–30 ms, the rate at which the spectral changes take place in vowels (monophthongs) is slower, less dynamic and more steady (Stevens, 1980). Rapid transitions between formants also give important information about the identity of unfolding speech sounds, such as the difference between *date* and *gate*, which is dependent on both the spectral information in the word-initial burst and on the following dynamic formant transitions marking the unfolding diphthong (Hazan & Rosen, 1991).

Apart from a detailed analysis of sound, the auditory system must be able to handle noise and variability in the signal, with the objective of extracting meaning from the acoustic sound waves reaching our ears. We regularly hear speech in wildly differing contexts and from different speakers, meaning that it is highly variable, and words and speech sounds are almost never heard out of the context of surrounding speech sounds. In quiet conditions, speech intelligibility is relatively intact even when spectral information is reduced and only envelope information is preserved (Loizou et al., 1999; Shannon et al., 1995), but speech in the presence of background noise may require more fine-structure information in order to be intelligible (Qin & Oxenham, 2003; Shamma & Lorenzi, 2013).

While the continuous signal proceeds in a 'left-to-right' fashion, the system transforms the signal through non-linear, parallel processes in which the perception of individual speech sounds is ultimately influenced by context at different levels. In this way, perception is driven by our experience with acoustic stimuli: it is *active* (Bajcsy, 1988; Helmholtz, 1878/1971). For example, syntactic boundaries between words are not necessarily marked by silences in the acoustic signal (see examples in Figure 2), but listeners nevertheless analyse phrases as perceptual units, as shown by experiments where listeners erroneously report hearing superimposed clicks at syntactic boundaries (Fodor & Bever, 1965; Holmes & Forster, 1972). The listener thus contributes perceptual structure to the signal, based on experience and rules of a particular language (Fodor & Bever, 1965). Identical acoustic signals can be perceived as different phonemes depending on context, and instances of the same phonetic category also vary in their physical properties within speakers (Allen et al., 2003; R. S. Newman et al., 2001). For example, if we consider the formant frequencies of the speech sound /d/ as in *date*, the acoustics are so strongly influenced by the following vowel that it is impossible to find one definitive acoustic correlate that sets the sound apart as a /d/ (Liberman et al., 1954). Studies using synthesised tone glissandos closely matching formant frequencies and transitions confirm that there is no simple psychoacoustic mapping between spectrotemporal properties and phonetic perception (Klatt & Shattuck, 1974).

A common source of context-dependent signal variance that the system must be able to handle is *coarticulation*, where the phonetic context – surrounding speech sounds – leads to the realisation of an allophonic (non-phonemic) variant of the intended speech sound. Since our articulators take time to shift between different configurations, articulatory gestures flow into and modify one another. For example, velar stops are articulated more frontally before a front vowel like /i/, and more towards the back of the mouth before a back vowel like /u/ (Öhman, 1966), while lip spreading or rounding influence the frequency content of a fricative like /s/ in *see* and *Sue* respectively: in *Sue*, the spectral energy of the fricative noise is lower, creating an anticipatory cue to the degree of round-edness of the upcoming vowel (Lulaci et al., 2022; Schreiber & McMurray, 2019). The perception of unvoiced stops similarly differs depending on the subsequent vowel: identical noise bursts are identified as /p/ if they precede /i/ or /u/, but as /k/ if they precede /a/ (Liberman, Delattre, & Cooper, 1952). Conversely, the second vowel in *Henry* is darker than that in *Henley* in Standard Southern British English, due to a lowering of F2 and F3 under influence from the consonant /ɹ/ (Local & Kelly, 1986). Coarticulatory effects are not restricted to immediately adjacent speech sounds but can spread through entire syllables and even further ahead in an utterance. At the level of the syllable, information about syllable-final voicing is available as early as in a syllable-initial phoneme, such as in the words *lack* and *lag*, where voiced codas are preceded by longer vowels with lower F1 and higher F2, as well as a darker and longer syllable-initial /l/ in British English (Hawkins & Nguyen, 2004). Over even longer timespans, anticipatory effects of an /ɹ/ can be heard up to five syllables, or one second, before the speech sound is heard, such as in a sentence like *we heard it might be ram* (Heid & Hawkins, 2000). It has been suggested that coarticulation may serve a communicative function in speech (Whalen, 1990), including over longer timespans or domains (West, 1999).

The extent of coarticulation between neighbouring sounds varies across languages (Manuel, 1999). For example, in English, the word *bank* is realised with the voiced velar nasal /ŋ/ under influence of the velar /k/. This type of coarticulatory process can either be optional or obligatory within and between languages. In Russian, the similar word банка (/banka/, 'jar') is realised with the voiced dental nasal /n/ with no effect of the velar stop, whereas, in English *bank*, this assimilation is obligatory. Listeners take advantage of their language experience and knowledge to account for how phonemes are actually realised in speech and to process the signal accurately. This mechanism is important since there is not necessarily any one-to-one mapping from formant frequency or spectral content to phoneme or sound identity, or between sound and perception: a *lack of invariance* (Liberman et al., 1967); a many-to-one mapping which the auditory perception system needs to achieve. For example, the perception of stops such as [b] and glides such as [w] is dependent on the duration of the following vowel, where a longer subsequent vowel is more likely to lead to the perception of a stop (J. L. Miller & Liberman, 1979), while vowels embedded in consonant-vowel-consonant (CVC) contexts are perceived differently depending on the spectral content of the surrounding speech sounds (Lindblom & Studdert-Kennedy, 1967).

If the system had no mechanism to compensate for sources of variance in the speech signal, perception would prove difficult. We thus need to create *perceptual constancy* across speakers and contexts (Kuhl, 1979; Summerfield, 1981). One of the most important solutions to the lack of invariance is *categorical perception*. The brain is able to generalise and find patterns across exemplars to form functionally equivalent categories. This is demonstrated by the fact that listeners find it easier to discriminate sounds that lie on opposite sides of a phoneme boundary, that is, between categories, as compared to sounds that belong to the same phoneme category (Liberman, Harris, Hoffman, & Griffith, 1957). Thus, while speech sounds vary in their acoustic, subphonemic realisation for a number of reasons, they are ultimately perceived as distinct categories of sounds. Since the main aim of the listener is to distinguish one word from another as quickly and as efficiently as possible, this is a crucial mechanism. For example, given synthesised tokens ranging from *ba* to *da*, listeners will report an abrupt change from one category to another, without reporting sounds as belonging to ambiguous or in-between categories. The categorical perception effect is stronger for consonants than vowels, which tend to be perceived in a more continuous and less categorical manner (Fry et al., 1962), suggesting that listeners are sensitive to finer distinctions in vowels. Since phoneme categories and category boundaries are by definition language-specific, so is categorical perception. Thus, in a language where *low* and *row* – such as Japanese – are not heard as different words, the sounds /l/ and /r/ are perceived as variants of the same sounds: they belong to the same category (Goto, 1971; Miyawaki et al., 1975). Categorical perception is also influenced by the phoneme inventory of the specific language, that is, how crowded the phoneme space is for certain categories of sounds. For example, phoneme-detection tasks have shown that if a language has many fricatives, like Polish, detection of fricatives in nonsense words is slower and less accurate. If a language has many vowels, like English, vowel detection is similarly impacted, and so on (Wagner & Ernestus, 2008).

However, phonetic categories are not immutable, and the compensation-for-coarticulation mechanism can shift phoneme category boundaries under a large number of conditions, at both lower and higher levels of processing (Repp & Liberman, 1987). Thus, at the level of individual speech sounds, listeners hear ambiguous stops ranging between /t/ and /k/ as more like /k/ following the fricative /s/, but as /t/ following /ʃ/, due to listeners' knowledge of the influence on the vocal tract configuration of lip spreading (as in /s/) and rounding (as in /ʃ/), as well as its effect on neighbouring speech sounds (Mann & Repp, 1981). Category adjustments also occur at the word and sentence levels. In the lexical domain, an ambiguous sound between /d/ and /t/ is more likely to be reported by English listeners as /t/ before /iːk/, but as /d/ before /iːp/. This is because *teak* and *deep* are words in English, whereas /diːk/ and /tiːp/ are not, showing a biasing effect of the contents of the listener's mental lexicon on phoneme categorisation, known as the *Ganong* effect: the tendency to perceive an ambiguous sound as a phoneme that could complete a real word rather than a nonword (Ganong, 1980). At the sentence level, the semantics of a preceding sentence lead to sounds between /b/ and /p/ being reported as /p/ in *She likes to jog along the -ath* but as /b/ in *She ran hot water for the -ath* (J. L. Miller, Green, & Schermer, 1984). In addition to these types of contexts, we must also be able to adapt to the physiology of individual speakers, as well as variations in pronunciation and dialects. We adapt to these variations in speech rapidly and efficiently. When hearing a word with ambiguous formant frequency in the vowel, our vowel percept is influenced by the spectral content of a preceding sentence, taking into account the physiology of the speaker's vocal tract (Broadbent, Ladefoged, & Lawrence, 1956; Ladefoged & Broadbent, 1957). We also adapt to deviations in the realisation of phonemes, allowing us to comprehend speakers with a different accent or even temporary differences in pronunciation (Norris, McQueen, & Cutler, 2003).

As a general principle in the auditory system, the immediate *contrast* between neighbouring sounds plays an important role in category adjustment (Diehl, Elman, & McCusker, 1978). Indeed, the basic function of speech segments in spoken language is to separate and differentiate sounds from each other, making them distinctive (Jakobson, Fant, & Halle, 1961). As Broadbent et al. (1956) and Ladefoged and Broadbent (1957) showed, the perception of vowels with ambiguous formant frequencies – for example, between *bit* and *bet* – is influenced by the spectral content of a preceding sentence (*Please say what this word is*). Specifically, when the introductory sentence had relatively low F1, a target word was perceived as a word with relatively *high* F1 (*bet*), while if the preceding context had higher F1, the word was perceived as *bit*, which has a relatively *low* F1 frequency. In more immediate contexts, following a voiced consonant with a *high* frequency content such as /d/ – or indeed a sine-wave non-speech analogue with similar acoustic properties – the subsequent vowel is more likely to be heard as a vowel with a *low* F2 (/ʌ/). Conversely, a vowel following a low-frequency consonant such as /b/ is more likely to be perceived as the high-F2 vowel /ɛ/ (Holt, Lotto, & Kluender, 2000). The frequency of preceding non-speech sine wave tones can also influence the perception of subsequent stops, with a subsequent sound being perceived as being lower in frequency as a function of increasing frequency in the preceding sound (Lotto & Kluender, 1998). Furthermore, when two similar consonants occur successively, an ambiguous consonant – for example, between /b/ and /d/ – is more likely to be perceived as having a posterior place of articulation when it is preceded by a consonant with an anterior place of articulation. Thus, the contrast between the two sounds is perceptually enhanced by the auditory system (Repp, 1978). Similarly, listeners are more likely to report hearing synthesised ambiguous stop consonants on a /d-g/ continuum as the velar stop /ga/ after /al/ but more likely to report the dental stop /da/ after /ar/ (Mann, 1980). The syllable /al/ has a more frontal place of articulation than /ar/. Consequently, with a lifetime of exposure to coarticulatory assimilation effects on native-language speech sounds, listeners expect stops following /l/ to be produced with a more forward place of articulation than those following /r/. Listeners also know that lip rounding in anticipation of an upcoming speech sound lowers the spectral frequency of a preceding fricative. When presented with an ambiguous sound between /s/ and /ʃ/, the sound is more likely to be heard as /s/ before a rounded vowel like /u/ (Mann & Repp, 1980). If this were not the case, the lower spectral frequency brought about by coarticulation could lead to the erroneous perception of a /ʃ/. This process of perceptual compensation – the strength of which can vary across listeners (Yu & Lee, 2014) – is influenced by the listener's native phonology and the transitional probabilities of the language (Pitt & McQueen, 1998), as well as basic auditory perception mechanisms, with a resulting decrease in the perceptual difference between canonical and assimilated speech sounds (Kang, Johnson, & Finley, 2016; Mitterer, Csépe, & Blomert, 2006). The system thus combines linguistic biases and acoustic knowledge to maximise perceptual contrast between speech sounds to account and compensate for these effects and give rise to a percept that can be influenced by both spectral content and attributes of the phonetic context (Kingston et al., 2014).

The brain's ability to perceive speech sounds in a categorical manner does not mean that we are insensitive to subphonemic detail, especially if that detail is perceptually useful. In fact, even in categorical perception tasks, subphonemic information is still available to the listener at the neural level, suggesting that both continuous and categorical representations may be active in parallel

(Beach et al., 2021; Dehaene-Lambertz et al., 2005). Thus, while speech sounds are realised differently depending on the surrounding phonetic context, and we can use our linguistic knowledge to compensate for this fact, we also take advantage of these variations during speech perception. The vowels in the English words *job* and *jog* contain subphonemic information about the place of articulation of the upcoming stop, meaning that the words become distinct even before the end of the vowel (Marslen-Wilson & Warren, 1994; McQueen, Norris, & Cutler, 1999) (see Figure 3). Listeners make use of this type of coarticulatory information to make word recognition more efficient and to rule potential similar-sounding competing words out of contention. It also allows the processor to retain information that may be useful in cases where an initial interpretation of the word turns out to be incorrect (McMurray et al., 2009).

In English, regressive assimilation can cause phrases like *freight bearer* to be produced as [freɪpbɛrə] rather than [freɪtbɛrə], with labial features spreading backwards from the /b/ in *bearer*. However, listeners still report hearing a /t/,

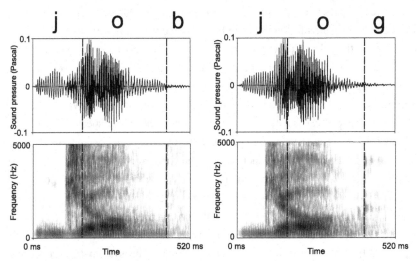

Figure 3 Waveforms and spectrograms for the words *job* (left) and *jog* (right), produced by an adult speaker of Northern British English. Vertical dashed lines indicate approximate segment boundaries. Coarticulation in the vowel is brought about by the articulators moving to produce either a labial or velar stop. In this example, there were no differences in mean vowel F1 frequency, but F2 and F3 were significantly lower on average in the vowel leading up to the release of *jog* as compared to *job*. Listeners take advantage of formant transitions and other subphonemic information in spoken-word recognition (Marslen-Wilson & Warren, 1994; McQueen et al., 1999).

albeit more slowly than in a canonical, non-assimilated version of the phrase. Thus, the auditory system helps the listeners to rapidly restore assimilated phonemes with little effort at an early prelexical stage (Gaskell & Marslen-Wilson, 1998; Mitterer & Blomert, 2003). Bringing lexical, semantic and other expectations to bear, listeners can even restore phonemes that have been masked or fully replaced by a noise burst or cough (R. M. Warren, 1970), provided that the burst is spectrally similar to the replaced sound (Samuel, 1981a, 1981b; R. M. Warren, 1984). This is extremely useful, given that we often hear speech in noisy conditions. Phoneme restoration is thus the effect of hearing a speech sound instead of the noise, given enough ambiguity, such as the medial /s/ in *legislatures* being replaced by or overlaid with noise in a sentence like *The state governors met with the respective legislatures convening in the capital city* (Samuel, 1981a, 1981b; R. M. Warren, 1970). In fact, listeners find it difficult to even locate the noise in a subsequently presented written version of the sentence (R. M. Warren, 1970), illustrating the strength of the effect.

In conclusion, while subphonemic information is available and actively used by the listener in speech perception, the auditory system performs a 'normalisation' as it transforms the continuous auditory input into discrete behaviourally and linguistically relevant categories. Categorical perception constitutes a solution to the variance problem, and malleable speech sound categories allow us to adjust to sound differences caused by factors ranging from individual speaker physiology or circumstance to phonetic context, distinguishing discrete words in the signal to ultimately lead to speech comprehension.

4.1 Prediction in Speech Perception and Spoken-Word Recognition

It has long been suggested that we do not just passively perceive the world. Rather, we actively but *unconsciously infer* the likely causes of the input, something which was originally discussed in relation to cognitive optical illusions that we cannot help but be tricked by (Helmholtz, 1867). Through unconscious inference, we construct and constantly update 'hypotheses' about the world. These are based on an internal model of how the world works, and we process input with respect to those hypotheses, creating structure in our perceived reality by combining the input with our knowledge and assumptions, presumably stored as statistical distributions (Leonard & Chang, 2014). Our perception and behaviour can thus operate on prior probabilities based on past experience and can, in this way, be *predictive*, analogously to a curve fitted to extant and expected data points, helping us fill in the blanks in partial or incomplete data using *top-down* modulation throughout the neural hierarchy (Asilador & Llano, 2020). This is supported by the fact that the majority of input connections to the primary auditory cortex originate in areas further up in the hierarchy (see Section 5.2). It is important to note, however, that unlikely perceptions do indeed occur, meaning that we cannot always simply accept the most likely hypothesis as true (Gregory, 1980). It has been proposed that the brain approximates *Bayes' theorem* or Bayesian inference (Bayes, 1763; Hohwy, 2020), which, put simply, provides the conditional probability of an event (such as encountering a particular spoken word), or the likelihood of a hypothesis being true, given the evidence or prior information. In perception, a central problem lies in the fact that the same sensory effect may have many potential different sources, and data can be noisy or ambiguous. Using Bayesian inference, bottom-up sensory information can be combined with prior information – including from the linguistic and communicative context – to arrive at the most likely causes of the sensory data and achieve optimal word recognition, that is, to recognise words as quickly as possible given an acceptable level of accuracy (Norris & McQueen, 2008). This assumption of optimality has led to entities using Bayesian decision theory being referred to as 'ideal observers' (Geisler, 2011; Geisler & Kersten, 2002). This is not to say that human perform-ance is always optimal, but the assumption instead provides a starting point for building explanatory theories and models, based on observations of deviations from optimality by human listeners. A related model commonly used to explain neural processing is *predictive coding* (Rao & Ballard, 1999). Predictive coding postulates that the brain generates models of the external world and updates them when new information violates expectations, generating a *prediction error*, which is the difference between sensory input and the prediction, that is, the 'news-worthy' information that cannot be predicted (Friston, 2018). The system then converges on the response that best explains the current input (Rao & Ballard, 1999). Thus, instead of representing the input directly, the brain can process the prediction error, making processing more efficient. The goal of the system is to minimise prediction error in the long run, allowing for unsupervised learning and inference, to constitute a solution to the problem of multiple potential causes of perceptual data (Hohwy, 2020). Through predictive coding, the brain has been proposed to predict input across the linguistic and neural hierarchies over multiple timescales (Caucheteux, Gramfort, & King, 2023).

In spoken-word recognition, an important source of prior information is word frequency, that is, how often a particular word occurs in speech. More frequent words like *cat* are more easily recognised than less frequent words, such as *vat* (Howes, 1957; Pollack, Rubenstein, & Decker, 1960; Savin, 1963), which is almost fifty times less frequent (Balota et al., 2007). The use of word frequency as prior information has been proposed to scale with ambiguity and noise: the more ambiguous the input, the more prior information exerts an influence (Norris & McQueen, 2008). In this general sense, prediction in speech perception and spoken-word recognition is a mechanism through which our beliefs are constantly updated as more data arrives. For example, the Ganong effect – lexical effects on phoneme categorisation (see Section 4) – can be explained by the interaction of pre-lexical and lexical information according to Bayesian principles (Norris, McQueen, & Cutler, 2016). At a more general level, word frequency provides a wide range of possible outcomes – a *weak prior* – while sentence context can conversely be highly constraining: the sentence onset *the cat sat on the* . . . may lead to the strong expectation of *mat*, while *he ate a* . . . is less constraining (Norris et al., 2016). Indeed, multiple words can become probable at the same time. At shorter timescales, incoming phonemes likewise provide prior information as regards the rest of the word, widening or narrowing probability distributions of possible outcomes (Friston et al., 2021; Gagnepain, Henson, & Davis, 2012; Roll et al., 2023; Söderström & Cutler, 2023). According to predictive coding models of word recognition, lexical candidates compete by making incompatible predictions of upcoming speech sounds and suppressing prediction errors from their neighbours (Gagnepain et al., 2012; Spratling, 2008).

As a way to explain why the brain extracts meaning from speech with such apparent ease, predictive processing has been postulated at all levels of speech perception and comprehension – from sentence contexts to specific phonological or lexical predictions – and it remains a widely researched and discussed topic. For example, in conversational turn-taking (Sacks, Schegloff, & Jefferson, 1974), speakers take on average 200 milliseconds – a mere fifth of a second – to transition between turns (Stivers et al., 2009). This is despite the fact that it takes much longer to plan and produce even short utterances, suggesting that mental processes must overlap (Levinson & Torreira, 2015). Crucially, the speed at which this happens also implies that some type of prediction is taking place: listeners can use a number of cues in the signal to anticipate the end of a turn (see A. S. Meyer (2023) for a review). This appeal to predictive processing is similar to arguments made in the context of speech shadowing, where speakers can repeat speech at speeds – 250 milliseconds or less between hearing and repeating – that strongly suggest a predictive influence from higher-order syntactic, semantic or pragmatic contexts (Chistovich, 1960; Marslen-Wilson, 1973, 1985). A sentence context can thus be used to pre-activate the semantic features of expected sentence-final words in a graded fashion (Federmeier & Kutas, 1999; Federmeier et al., 2002), and the phonological structure (DeLong, Urbach, & Kutas, 2005) or acoustic features

(Broderick, Anderson, & Lalor, 2019) of words can be predicted based on context or lexical knowledge (Brodbeck, Hong, & Simon, 2018). Furthermore, the endings of words can be predicted based on the 'micro-context' of word onsets (Roll et al., 2017; Roll et al., 2023; Söderström & Cutler, 2023; Söderström et al., 2016; Söderström et al., 2017; Söderström, Horne, & Roll, 2017).

5 Structure and Function of the Auditory System

5.1 From the Cochlea to Auditory Nuclei

When sound waves reach the cochlea in the inner ear, the mechanical energy is converted to electrical energy that can be analysed by the nervous system (Hudspeth, 1997). The cochlea performs a spectral decomposition of the signal, and this transformed acoustic information is sent on in the form of electrical signals – sequences of action potentials, or spikes – from the cochlea in several parallel streams through cochlear ganglion cells and the *auditory nerve* (or cochlear nerve). The physical properties of the incoming sound are encoded through the temporal and spatial distribution of action potentials (Rouiller, 1997; Shamma, 2001). For example, increased sound intensity leads to an increase in nerve impulses ascending the auditory nerve (Galambos & Davis, 1943), and different frequency bands are processed in different parts of the basilar membrane in the cochlea (Fletcher, 1940). Signals are sent through to several auditory nuclei (a nucleus is a cluster of neurons) and areas in the brainstem and midbrain, including the olivary complex in the brainstem, the inferior colliculus in the midbrain, and on to the thalamus, which relays the information to auditory areas in the cerebral cortex higher up in the processing hierarchy (Huffman & Henson, 1990) (see Figure 4).

These parallel streams are responsible for conveying different aspects or features of the acoustic signal, such as pitch or spectral information, as well as the onsets and offsets of sounds. The subcortical detection and extraction of these acoustic features allows for cortical structures to subsequently merge them into more complete acoustic objects (Nelken, 2004). Several layers of this hierarchy are further defined by *tonotopy*, meaning that there is spatial separation in how different frequencies of sound are transmitted and processed (Romani, Williamson, & Kaufman, 1982). For example, the cochlea is organised so that low-frequency components of the sound are processed at one end, with increasingly higher frequencies being processed along the length of the cochlea towards the other end. This is then reflected in the fact that fibres from the low-frequency end – the apex – terminate at different parts of the neuron clusters connected to the cochlea – the cochlear nuclei – as compared to fibres

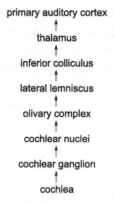

primary auditory cortex
↑
thalamus
↑
inferior colliculus
↑
lateral lemniscus
↑
olivary complex
↑
cochlear nuclei
↑
cochlear ganglion
↑
cochlea

Figure 4 Illustration of the signal path from the cochlea to the primary auditory cortex. This heavily simplified figure does not show any differences in lateralisation between the two brain hemispheres, and it does not show any descending (efferent) pathways (only ascending/afferent).

from the high-frequency part of the cochlea. The tonotopic organisation of the system ensures that a representation or map of the cochlea is maintained all the way from subcortical networks to the cerebral cortex. This spatial organisation of nerve fibres is sometimes referred to as a *place code*, while the *rate* or *frequency code* refers to the frequency of a signal being reflected in the spiking rate of neurons.

5.2 Subcortical Networks and the Extraction of Acoustic Features of Speech

As the signal travels from the cochlea, subcortical networks – located in the hierarchy between the cochlea and primary auditory cortex (see Figure 4, Section 5.1) – play an important role in extracting and transforming the features that are crucial for successful perception of sound and speech. At early stages in this ascending auditory pathway, the firing of auditory nerve fibres closely represents both the fine and coarse structure of complex sounds. Thus, the temporal and frequency information of speech is represented in auditory nerve activity, so that certain fibres respond more strongly to certain frequencies while temporal modulations in the signal are represented in the latency, timing and firing rate of the neural response (Joris & Yin, 1992; Rose et al., 1967; Young & Sachs, 1979). For example, modulations over time in the neural response directly represent temporal features of speech such as voice-onset time (Young, 2008). Thus, it has been suggested that in the early auditory system, the timing of neuronal spiking underlies the processing of consonant sounds while the fine-structure detail in vowel sounds is represented by spiking rates of neurons synchronising with the signal (Perez et al., 2013). The electric *auditory brainstem response* (ABR) can be tracked over time using EEG electrodes on the scalp (Jewett & Williston, 1971; Jewett, Romano, & Williston, 1970). Short, non-periodic stimuli elicit transient responses, while periodic stimuli (such as vowels) elicit sustained responses that are part of the ABR. The ABR is commonly used in clinical settings to test auditory function using simple click sounds, but it has also been widely used to track brainstem processing of speech sounds, where it has been found to reflect speech-specific information such as fundamental and formant frequencies, as well as syllable structure (Greenberg, 1980; Moushegian, Rupert, & Stillman, 1973; Russo et al., 2004; Worden & Marsh, 1968; Young & Sachs, 1979).

As the signals converge and are integrated to begin to form percepts, there is a gradual decrease in the precision of the representation as we reach higher levels of the system. Neurons in the auditory nerve may phase-lock to information at up to 10,000 Hz, corresponding to the fine structure of speech (Heinz, Colburn, & Carney, 2001) and neurons in the cochlear nuclei synchronise with signals at rates of hundreds or thousands of cycles per second (Rhode & Greenberg, 1994), whereas neurons at subsequent higher stages of the hierarchy – from the inferior colliculus to the thalamus and on to the primary auditory cortex – operate at increasingly slower levels of stimulus synchronisation (Bartlett & Wang, 2007; Liang et al., 2002; Rees & Palmer, 1989; Yin et al., 2011) as representations also become more complex.

At this point, it is important to note that, while this simplified illustration of the auditory system proceeds in a hierarchical, linear fashion from cochlea to cortex – also mostly overlooking hemispheric differences between the left and right sides of the brain – the flow of processing from the ear to the brain is not simply unidirectional. Moreover, many neural responses represent the speech signal non-linearly (Christianson, Sahani, & Linden, 2008; David et al., 2009) and seldom isomorphically. That is, one-to-one mappings between the input and neural representation appear to be rare, apart from the level of the early auditory system (Repp, 1988; Young, 2008). Recall that perception is an active process (Bajcsy, 1988; Friston, 2005; Helmholtz, 1867, 1878/1971) and thus we do not just hear, we *listen* (Friston et al., 2021). There are multiple two-way flows of information at all levels of the system, meaning that there are both *ascending* (afferent) pathways going towards the brain and *descending* (efferent) pathways carrying information back down through the auditory system, in several feedback loops from the cortex to subcortical structures, including the thalamus and inferior colliculus (Winer et al., 2002), as well as nuclei further down in the hierarchy, such as the olivary complex (Coomes & Schofield, 2004) and cochlear nucleus (Held, 1893; Schofield & Coomes, 2006; Weedman & Ryugo,

1996a, 1996b). The pathways from the auditory cortex all the way down to the cochlea are often referred to as *corticofugal* projections. In fact, roughly one-third of inputs to the primary auditory cortex originate in and ascend from subcortical areas, while two-thirds – the majority – are descending signals from cortical areas higher up in the hierarchy (Diamond, Jones, & Powell, 1969; Scheich et al., 2007). Descending signals serve to sharpen and tune the response of subcortical neurons (Suga, 2008) to filter and control incoming acoustic information, and the longest feedback signals go back as far as the hair cells in the cochlea, where they continue to play an important role in speech perception (Froehlich et al., 1990; Garinis, Glattke, & Cone, 2011; Huffman & Henson, 1990; Luo et al., 2008). At the level of the cochlea, signals descending through the system from the olivary complex also help to protect the cochlea and its hair cells from traumatic effects caused by loud sounds (Guinan, 2006; Taranda et al., 2009). This descending pathway is modulated by *attention*, the mechanism that allows listeners to focus on behaviourally relevant stimuli (Galbraith & Arroyo, 1993; Giard et al., 1994; Petersen & Posner, 2012). Attention increases the signal-to-noise ratio (Mertes, Johnson, & Dinger, 2019), sharpens the response to speech in noise and facilitates cocktail-party speech perception – the ability to focus on one stimulus in the presence of others competing for attention – prior to cortical processing (Cherry, 1953; Festen & Plomp, 1990; Price & Bidelman, 2021).

The importance of peripheral subcortical networks for speech perception has been highlighted by research into patients with auditory neuropathy. These patients have minimal cochlear and cognitive deficits but have great difficulty understanding speech. One such patient, an eleven-year-old girl, perceived speakers as sounding 'weird, like spacemen' (Starr et al., 1991). This was marked by difficulty in distinguishing vowel sounds, but a relatively unaffected ability to distinguish words based on high-frequency consonants. Auditory neuropathy appears to affect the temporal precision of neural coding and transmission in the auditory nerve, with less effect on percepts based on frequency or intensity. A larger study of twenty-one patients further corroborated the impact of auditory nerve timing deficits on speech perception (Zeng et al., 2005), finding a decreased ability to detect transient and rapidly changing sounds. In addition, pitch discrimination was found to be impaired below 4 kHz, and temporal processing deficits further manifested as difficulties in separating successively occurring sounds and detecting both slow and fast temporal modulations, as well as gaps between sounds. These types of temporal mechanisms perform important functions in speech perception. A relatively slow temporal modulation such as voice-onset time (VOT) – the time between the release of a stop consonant and the onset of voicing – is an important cue to the difference between the voiced and voiceless consonants in *pa* and *ba* in English (Lisker & Abramson, 1964), where a gap shorter than 30 ms leads to the perception of voicing and a longer gap signals voicelessness (Wood, 1976). Thus, while a sound sequence like *ama* does not contain any perceptible gaps, *aba* contains a voice-onset gap which may be a useful cue to phoneme identification. Listeners with normal hearing can detect gaps of only a couple of milliseconds (Fitzgibbons, 1984), but a perceptual threshold of around 30 ms has been posited with regard to speech phenomena like voice-onset time (Pastore & Farrington, 1996). In the subcortical auditory system, circuits in the ventral cochlear nucleus (VCN) involving temporally precise and sensitive octopus cells detect and track acoustic onsets and periodicity (Ferragamo & Oertel, 2002; Golding, Ferragamo, & Oertel, 1999), as well as synchrony (Oertel et al., 2000), suggesting an important role of these circuits in the processing of VOT and similar, relatively slow, temporal modulations in speech perception. Octopus cells also synchronise strongly to faster amplitude envelope modulations (Rhode, 1994; Rhode & Greenberg, 1994) and thus appear to be involved in the processing of fundamental frequency and vowel-type formant information (Rhode, 1998). Ascending the pathway, octopus cells target areas of the superior olivary complex – the first point of binaural convergence in the auditory system (Walton & Burkard, 2001) – as well as the lateral lemniscus (Felix II et al., 2017).

Many acoustic features of speech have been analysed through multiple afferent pathways in the brainstem when the signal reaches the *inferior colliculus*, an important nucleus located in the midbrain. All ascending auditory pathways converge here, and it also receives descending information from the thalamus and cortex (Rouiller, 1997). Processing in the inferior colliculus is more complex than in systems preceding it in the peripheral auditory system, but less so than in the cortex (Portfors & Sinex, 2005). Information about the timing and intensity of sounds reaching the ears at subtly different times is processed and sent to the superior colliculus, where it is used to localise sounds in space. The inferior colliculus contains neurons sensitive to amplitude- and frequency-modulated sounds (Rees & Møller, 1987; Rodríguez, Read, & Escabí, 2010; Schuller, 1979), as well as sound duration and offset (Casseday, Ehrlich, & Covey, 1994, 2000; Ehrlich, Casseday, & Covey, 1997) and gap detection (Walton, Frisina, & O'Neill, 1998). Voice-onset time appears to be represented in a similar fashion to the auditory nerve, that is, through a pause in neuronal spiking corresponding to the VOT (Young, 2008). The inferior colliculus plays a crucial role in the process of filtering and sharpening the signal, as well as compensating for the effects of reverberation on the amplitude envelope of the speech signal (Slama & Delgutte, 2015; Suga, 1995), for example when the system perceives vowels such as /a/ and /i/ (Sayles, Stasiak, & Winter, 2016). This early filtering and compensation system appears to help the primary auditory cortex further up in the hierarchy fulfil important functions, such as processing speech sounds as robust and invariant categories in conditions marked by noise or reverberation (Mesgarani et al., 2014), which may occur in a loud restaurant or cocktail party where we may hear many people speaking at once (Cherry, 1953).

5.3 From Subcortical to Cortical Processing of Speech

From the inferior colliculus, signals are relayed through the medial geniculate body – the auditory part of the thalamus – and on to the auditory cortex, which is located in the temporal lobe of the brain. It takes ten to twenty milliseconds for the acoustic information to be transferred from the cochlea to the auditory cortex (Eldredge & Miller, 1971; Rupp et al., 2002) and much acoustic processing has occurred before the signal reaches this point. It has been suggested that the detailed analysis of spectrotemporal features of speech is complete at the level of the inferior colliculus (Nelken et al., 2003) and the nature of the processing and representation of sound broadly changes as the signal reaches cortical areas (L. M. Miller et al., 2001). For example, the modulation transfer function of the auditory system – essentially its temporal resolution – is around ten times lower in cortical than subcortical structures (<100 Hz vs. ~1,000 Hz) (Joris & Yin, 1992; Kowalski, Depireux, & Shamma, 1996; Rhode & Greenberg, 1994; Schreiner & Urbas, 1986; Yin et al., 2011). The auditory cortex can be viewed as a bank of filters, arranged according to tonotopy, that responds to spectrotemporal modulations, so that sounds are decomposed through axes going from slow to fast temporal rates of modulation, and from narrow to broad scales of spectral modulation. Thus, while peripheral subcortical structures transform the acoustic signal to a time-frequency representation, the auditory cortex performs a more complex, joint spectrotemporal decomposition and analysis: just as the cochlea represents the sound wave at different frequencies, the auditory cortex represents the sound spectrogram at different resolutions (Chi, Ru, & Shamma, 2005). As a principle, it has been suggested that posterior/dorsal regions of the auditory cortex respond selectively to coarse spectral information with high temporal precision, while anterior/ventral regions encode fine-grained spectral information with low temporal precision (Santoro et al., 2014).

Representations also become more complex and categorical – invariant – as we reach higher stages in the hierarchy (Carruthers et al., 2015; Perez et al., 2013; Sharpee, Atencio, & Schreiner, 2011), such that cortical areas respond strongly to behaviourally meaningful categories of sounds rather than only general spectrotemporal properties. From the thalamus and primary auditory cortex onwards, it has been proposed that the brain thus operates primarily on complex, higher-order sound *objects* rather than basic acoustic features (Mesgarani et al., 2008; Nelken et al., 2003). Cortical responses are also malleable – or plastic – and change in the short or long term depending on behavioural or contextual requirements, as well as statistical regularities. Thus, cortical responses can change if required due to experience, an experimental task or expectation of a reward, that is, if something is behaviourally relevant (Fritz, Shamma, Elhilali, & Klein, 2003; Scheich et al., 2007). This allows for perceptual enhancement of degraded speech and enables more efficient perception (Holdgraf et al., 2016). In oddball paradigms, where stimuli appear with different probabilities of occurrence (see Section 3.2), more rare stimuli show stronger responses in the primary auditory cortex than common stimuli (Ulanovsky, Las, & Nelken, 2003), something which – combined with later processing stages (Schönwiesner et al., 2007) – is subsequently reflected in the mismatch negativity (MMN) ERP component on the scalp (Näätänen et al., 1978). These types of findings corroborate the idea that cortical responses are sensitive to behaviourally relevant and more abstract representations of sound in a way that those found lower down in the hierarchy are not (Chechik & Nelken, 2012; Nelken, 2008). Another feature of processing that is typical for the cerebral cortex – especially as we move beyond primary auditory areas – is speech specificity or selectivity, meaning that neurons may respond preferentially to speech over non-speech stimuli (Scott & Johnsrude, 2003). This may be driven by the particular nature of speech, which is acoustically complex as seen in envelope variability and the structure and transitions of formants and so on (Hullett et al., 2016).

The earliest stage of the processing hierarchy in the cerebral cortex lies in the primary auditory cortex, more specifically in the medial part of an area known as the transverse temporal or *Heschl's gyrus* (Morosan et al., 2001), comprising Brodmann areas 41 and 42 (Brodmann, 1909). Its importance for speech perception was noted as early as the nineteenth century when Adolf Kussmaul and Ludwig Lichtheim connected damage to the area with an auditory comprehension disorder known as pure word deafness (Pandya et al., 2015). While this area also responds to unmodulated spectral non-speech noise (Hickok & Poeppel, 2004), Heschl's gyrus appears to contain mechanisms that are specialised for speech processing. In this role, the auditory cortex responds strongly to amplitude- and frequency-modulated sounds (Ding & Simon, 2009; Liégeois-Chauvel et al., 2004) and transforms acoustic features from simple to more complex representations. Heschl's gyrus also plays a role in pitch processing

(De Angelis et al., 2018; Griffiths & Hall, 2012; Kumar et al., 2011). Certain parts of the primary auditory cortex respond preferentially to phonemes as compared to non-speech sounds, and it also encodes speaker-specific features as well as speaker-invariant categorical representations of phonemes, allowing us to achieve perceptual constancy of phoneme identity in processing (Khalighinejad et al., 2021; Town, Wood, & Bizley, 2018). These functions are crucial for speech processing since we need both to be able to distinguish and identify different speakers and to create abstract, speaker-invariant categories. Since there is variation in how speech sounds are pronounced and realised (see Section 4), we need to normalise the acoustic signal and create robust phonemic categories that are insensitive to acoustic variations, such as allophones. In this way, we can suppress information that may be perceptually irrelevant.

While the surrounding secondary auditory areas also exhibit more domain-general properties (Griffiths & Warren, 2002), a relative specialisation and sensitivity to speech sounds continues to define sound processing as we progress along the cortical hierarchy. Thus, the nearby supratemporal plane – comprising the planum polare, planum temporale and superior temporal gyrus (STG) – combines to encode the formant frequencies of vowels and spectrotemporal composition of consonants (Formisano et al., 2008; Näätänen et al., 1997; J. D. Warren, Jennings, & Griffiths, 2005), including extremely transient sounds such as consonantal stops (Obleser et al., 2007). It is also involved in abstract sublexical processing in speech perception (Hasson et al., 2007) and is sensitive to transitional probabilities between speech sounds or syllables and other statistical regularities, as is Heschl's gyrus (Leonard et al., 2015; McNealy, Mazziotta, & Dapretto, 2006; Roll et al., 2015; Söderström et al., 2017; Tobia et al., 2012; Tremblay, Baroni, & Hasson, 2013). Planum temporale completes the spectral envelope analysis and abstraction before further phoneme-level processing higher up in the temporal lobe (Kumar et al., 2007).

The primary auditory cortex connects through a cortico-cortical stream to the posterior part of the superior temporal gyrus (pSTG) (Brodmann, 1909; Brugge et al., 2003), which – in the left hemisphere of the brain – is traditionally considered as part of Wernicke's area (Binder, 2015; Bogen & Bogen, 1976). The pSTG, which is connected to but functionally distinct from Heschl's gyrus, is a core association area for acoustic processing and spectrotemporal analysis (Hickok & Poeppel, 2007; Howard et al., 2000). It has even been shown that spectrotemporal details of speech can be reconstructed using cortical neuro-electric data from the pSTG (Pasley et al., 2012). Brodmann (1909) defined the STG as area 22, and modern analyses of cell and receptor composition have been used to refine definitions of this area further (Morosan et al., 2005; Zachlod et al., 2020). A 'tuning' gradient runs across the length of the superior temporal gyrus so that pSTG specialises in speech varying fast over time – with high frequency but low spectral modulation – while the anterior part of the axis specialises in speech with slow temporal modulations but with higher spectral modulation. Thus, the posterior part is more specialised in phonemic processing, while temporally slow syllabic or prosodic processing occurs in the anterior part, towards the front of the brain (Hullett et al., 2016). The transformation of speech sounds to categorical phoneme representations thus emerges in Heschl's gyrus and continues onto the surface of the superior temporal gyrus (Chang et al., 2010; Formisano et al., 2008; Khalighinejad et al., 2021; Steinschneider et al., 2011). In fact, the entire inventory of American English phonemes has been mapped onto sites along the STG, with distinct neural populations sensitive to contrastive features such as place and manner of articulation, voicing and voice-onset time rather than to discrete phonemes, suggesting a complex, multidimensional mechanism that operates on the acoustic features that make up the phonemes and phonemic contrasts of a language (Chang et al., 2010; Mesgarani et al., 2014; Steinschneider et al., 2011).

The STG also performs a normalisation of these sound representations, adjusting for differences in individual voices so that speaker-independent meaning can be extracted from the spoken message (Sjerps et al., 2019). It can also perceptually restore phonemes (see Section 4) based on top-down input from frontal regions, at around 150 milliseconds after the onset of an ambiguous noise that replaces a phoneme within a word. This helps make processing robust to noisy conditions (Leonard et al., 2016), highlighting the important role that the STG plays in transforming sound to phonological representations and in the solution to the variance problem in speech perception. Categorical phonemic perception is also subserved by the *superior temporal sulcus* (STS), which lies lateral to and below Heschl's gyrus (Uppenkamp et al., 2006). At this point, according to the dual-route model of speech perception, the system diverges into the ventral and dorsal streams, with the ventral stream mapping sensory or phonological representations onto lexical conceptual representations (sound to meaning), and the dorsal stream responsible for mapping phonological representations onto articulatory motor representations (meaning to sound) (Hickok & Poeppel, 2007). The STS has been suggested to be part of a network with the middle temporal gyrus (MTG) that goes from phonological processing and the categorical perception of phonemes to their integration into higher-level semantic representations to drive speech comprehension, with the anterior portions of the STS being involved in the integration of phonemes into words

(DeWitt & Rauschecker, 2012; Liebenthal et al., 2005; Overath et al., 2015; Scott & Johnsrude, 2003). The posterior MTG is thus considered a lexical interface and storage of abstract word representations in the ventral stream, mapping sound to meaning (Davis & Gaskell, 2009; Gow, 2012; Hickok & Poeppel, 2000, 2004, 2007). The STS is sensitive to the higher-order word-recognition process of lexical competition – words or lexical candidates competing with each other for activation and recognition – in the form of lexical neighbourhood density (Luce & Pisoni, 1998; Okada & Hickok, 2006). The superior temporal gyrus is also involved in this process. Gagnepain et al. (2012) suggest a model whereby neurons in the STG represent the difference between predicted and heard speech sounds (see Section 4.1). In this way, lexical candidates compete by giving rise to incompatible predictions for which speech sounds will be heard next. Next to the posterior STG lies the *supramarginal gyrus* (SMG, BA40), with no sharp border between the regions with respect to cellular composition (Brodmann, 1909). An inferior parietal area traditionally viewed as part of Wernicke's area along with the STG, the supramarginal gyrus continues the higher-level categorical analysis of speech sounds together with the nearby angular gyrus (BA39) (Joanisse, Zevin, & McCandliss, 2007) and serves as an interface between phonetic and semantic representations for articulation in the dorsal stream (Gow, 2012). The supramarginal gyrus – along with frontal areas such as the inferior frontal gyrus – has also been found to exert top-down influence on lexical and phonemic processing in the STS and STG (Gow et al., 2008), and the SMG itself is subject to modulation from higher-level frontal areas (Gelfand & Bookheimer, 2003). The perception of categories in the supramarginal gyrus is driven by the selective amplification of key stimulus differences, that is, across phoneme boundaries, while differences treated as invariances (within-category) are suppressed (Raizada & Poldrack, 2007). Together, the supramarginal and angular gyri form the *inferior parietal lobule*, the area referred to by Norman Geschwind (1965a) as the 'association area of association areas' (see Section 2). The angular gyrus itself has been suggested to be at the top of a processing hierarchy in the retrieval and integration of semantic representations (Binder et al., 2009; Righi et al., 2010), and is also involved together with SMG in the active prediction of upcoming words (Willems et al., 2016) and word endings (Roll et al., 2017; Söderström et al., 2017).

Areas in the temporal and parietal lobes connect via a large network of white-matter pathways to each other and to frontal regions of the brain (Gow, 2012). The arcuate fasciculus, which has traditionally been considered to be the most important language-network connection, runs between Broca's and Wernicke's areas (H. C. Bastian, 1887; Dejerine, 1895). This tract contains a direct pathway between temporal and frontal regions, as well as two indirect pathways described using modern neuroimaging techniques. These indirect pathways connect the inferior parietal lobe – the supramarginal and angular gyri – to Broca's and Wernicke's areas, respectively. This suggests that a more complex anatomically and functionally dissociable white-matter network than has been traditionally assumed is involved in speech perception. The direct pathway has been suggested to mainly subserve phonological processing, with a more semantically oriented role for the indirect, inferior parietal pathway (Catani, Jones, & ffytche, 2005).

While much processing occurs in parallel at different levels of the linguistic and neural hierarchies (Beach et al., 2021; Gwilliams et al., 2022; Rauschecker & Scott, 2009), information can pass between temporal and frontal areas of the brain in ten to thirty milliseconds, as measured by the timing of early auditory ERP components (Matsumoto et al., 2004; Pulvermüller & Shtyrov, 2008; Pulvermüller et al., 2003). Similarly to descending corticofugal pathways from the primary auditory cortex influencing subcortical processing all the way down to the level of the cochlea (see Section 5.1), frontal areas of the brain play a crucial role in providing descending top-down modulations of processing in speech perception, mediating activity in areas such as the temporal and primary auditory cortices, and allowing us to attend to and predict stimuli that are relevant to behaviour (Braga, Wilson, Sharp, Wise, & Leech, 2013; Brass & von Cramon, 2004; Cope et al., 2017; Tzourio et al., 1997). Depending on the source of this top-down information, this can take place over tens or hundreds of milliseconds (i.e., in the case of phonemic processing) or seconds in the case of prosody, as well as longer timescales. There is thus a hierarchy of linguistic representations over a number of timescales in the brain, with higher-order predictions generated in frontal and associative areas (Wacongne et al., 2011). While the exact neural principles and mechanisms involved in top-down processing remain debated and widely researched, frontal areas have thus been proposed to play more abstract, decision-related roles in auditory processing (Binder, Liebenthal, Possing, Medler, & Ward, 2004; Scott & Johnsrude, 2003) and activity in prefrontal areas can influence processing at lower levels in the auditory hierarchy, such as the primary auditory cortex (Wang, Zhang, Zou, Luo, & Ding, 2019), and has been suggested to drive representational computations to achieve category invariance in perception (Myers, Blumstein, Walsh, & Eliassen, 2009). Recall that the superior temporal gyrus can process phoneme-replacing noise as phonetic information given a surrounding lexical context, so that a word like *fa[?]tor* can be perceived as *factor*, with the appropriate phoneme rapidly restored by the perceptual system.

To achieve this, the restoration in the temporal lobe is preceded by biasing predictive neural activity in frontal areas, particularly the left inferior frontal gyrus (Leonard et al., 2016). Similarly, being given explicit context information about upcoming ambiguous speech sounds, syllables or words helps us disambiguate and perceive these sounds (G. A. Miller, Heise, & Lichten, 1951; O'Neill, 1957), much like the implicit effect that preceding sounds or within-word context has on the perception of phonemes (Lotto & Kluender, 1998; Marslen-Wilson, 1975). In this way, a preceding stimulus or context – spoken language or written text – can provide disambiguating top-down information to bias the perception of subsequently presented degraded speech, and this use of prior information to disambiguate speech is also associated with activity in the inferior frontal gyrus, which lies at a high level of the auditory hierarchy (Sohoglu & Davis, 2016). This is in contrast with disambiguating *bottom-up* information, such as an increase in the perceptual detail in the auditory stimulus, which triggers activity in lower-level auditory areas in the superior temporal gyrus rather than frontal areas (Sohoglu et al., 2012). Importantly, the mediating connection between frontal and temporal regions allows both acoustic and linguistic information to interact as we process the phonemes of incoming words, and thus fuses phonetic and phonological information (Cope et al., 2023; Cope et al., 2017; Kim, Martino, & Overath, 2023; Overath & Lee, 2017). This occurs through spectral analyses of formant structures in loops between the primary auditory cortex and superior temporal gyrus and sulcus, which are modulated by signals from frontal areas such as the left inferior frontal gyrus.

The main goal of the speech perception and word recognition process is to establish what a spoken word is as quickly as possible, from sound waves entering our ears through to acoustic and linguistic analysis of the fleeting signal. We recognise words extremely rapidly: the brain can tell real and nonwords apart based on an incoming disambiguating speech sound as quickly as thirty to fifty milliseconds after phoneme onset, performing 'first pass' lexical processing in left temporal and frontal cortical circuits (MacGregor et al., 2012; Shtyrov & Lenzen, 2017). Speech perception is an active process through which combined bottom-up and top-down mechanisms allow us to consider information as soon as it becomes available and represent discrete, invariant, and categorically perceived phonemes, continuously resolving ambiguous information and integrating prior information with sensory signals – throughout the neural hierarchy from cochlea to cortex – as words unfold in time, to ultimately comprehend the speaker's message.

6 Directions for Future Research

Advances in our understanding of language and speech, as well as the brain, auditory system and experimental methodology, have propelled the fields of phonetics and neuroscience over the past century and a half. A parallel evolution in both fields has been necessary to reach the current levels of knowledge we have about how the brain processes spoken language. Neuroimaging techniques now allow temporal and spatial resolutions of neural processing at the millisecond and submillimetre scales. A slew of psycholinguistic methods developed over the past half-century are used to probe a wide range of detailed questions in language processing. Meanwhile, new statistical methods can provide more robust interpretations of both behavioural and neuroimaging data.

However, continued linguistic and neuroscientific theory and model-building are still crucial if we are to generate and constrain hypotheses to explain the actual data: not just *how* something works, but *why* it works the way it does (Norris & Cutler, 2021). This includes extending the experimental psycholinguistic endeavour to more languages so as to understand what linguistic phenomena are possible and how listeners take advantage of them in perception. Less-studied languages with particular lexical and morphosyntactic properties can be used to expand theories about both language and the brain, such as Welsh (Boyce, Browman, & Goldstein, 1987; Vaughan-Evans et al., 2014) or Iwaidja (Evans, 2000), spoken on Croker Island in northern Australia. In these languages, word-initial phonemes can change depending on syntactic context, something which will have implications for theories of lexical processing. The more specific and representative the linguistic and psycholinguistic description, the easier it is to create linking hypotheses together with the neurophysiologist and search for corresponding neural correlates, to ultimately create models that are consistent with both language and brain function. That being said, a phonetician does not necessarily have to be interested in neurobiology to use neuroimaging techniques to address empirical questions: one can study the mind without studying the brain. For example, in EEG studies, it is perfectly valid to use the presence of an MMN (see Section 3.2) to determine whether listeners can perceive a difference between two speech sounds, without addressing the potential neural generators of the MMN. Similarly, while the neural underpinnings of the N400 are widely researched and largely unknown, a larger N400 component in one condition is nevertheless a strong indication that a stimulus is perceived like a word (in contrast to a pseudoword), and so on. This may be less straightforward in fMRI, where the careless use of *reverse inference* – where a particular cognitive process is inferred from observed activity in a particular brain region – can lead to incorrect interpretations of the data (Hutzler, 2014; Poldrack, 2006). Similarly, one cannot understand brain function by simply knowing *where* something is processed: an understanding of the hierarchical and parallel neural systems and subsystems that underlie perception is necessary.

A key development is currently underway in the combination of linguistic and neural models with machine-learning and artificial intelligence techniques (see Section 3.3), as well as ongoing interdisciplinary collaborations between speech scientists and neuroscientists worldwide. This will benefit further research using both naturalistic speech and large-scale corpora of spoken language, and carefully controlled experimental paradigms and stimuli traditionally employed in psycholinguistic research. Models such as predictive coding keep spawning and constraining hypotheses regarding multiple facets of brain function (Friston, 2018), while the generation, content and temporal dynamics of predictions in the brain remain a fruitful subject of ongoing study: not just to answer how speech perception occurs, but also why it is usually so efficient.

References

Alho, K. (1995). Cerebral generators of mismatch negativity (MMN) and its magnetic counterpart (MMNm) elicited by sound changes. *Ear and Hearing*, *16*(1), 38–51.

Allen, J. S., Miller, J. L., & DeSteno, D. (2003). Individual talker differences in voice-onset-time. *The Journal of the Acoustical Society of America*, *113*(1), 544–52. https://doi.org/10.1121/1.1528172.

Asilador, A., & Llano, D. A. (2020). Top-down inference in the auditory system: Potential roles for corticofugal projections. *Frontiers in Neural Circuits*, *14*, 615259. https://doi.org/10.3389/fncir.2020.615259.

Baayen, R. H., Davidson, D. J., & Bates, D. M. (2008). Mixed-effects modeling with crossed random effects for subjects and items. *Journal of Memory and Language*, *59*(4), 390–412. https://doi.org/10.1016/j.jml.2007.12.005.

Bajcsy, R. (1988). Active perception. *Proceedings of the IEEE*, *76*(8), 966–1005. https://doi.org/10.1109/5.5968.

Balota, D. A., Yap, M. J., Cortese, M. J. et al. (2007). The english lexicon project. *Behavior Research Methods*, *39*(3), 445–59. https://doi.org/10.3758/bf03193014.

Barr, D. J., Levy, R., Scheepers, C., & Tily, H. J. (2013). Random effects structure for confirmatory hypothesis testing: Keep it maximal. *Journal of Memory and Language*, *68*(3), 255–78. https://doi.org/10.1016/j.jml.2012.11.001.

Bartlett, E. L., & Wang, X. (2007). Neural representations of temporally modulated signals in the auditory thalamus of awake primates. *Journal of Neurophysiology*, *97*(2), 1005–17. https://doi.org/10.1152/jn.00593.2006.

Bastian, H. C. (1887). On different kinds of aphasia, with special reference to their classification and ultimate pathology. *British Medical Journal*, *2*(1401), 985–90. https://doi.org/10.1136/bmj.2.1401.985.

Bastian, J., Eimas, P. D., & Liberman, A. M. (1961). Identification and discrimination of a phonemic contrast induced by silent interval. *The Journal of the Acoustical Society of America*, *33*(6), 842. https://doi.org/10.1121/1.1936842.

Bayes, T. (1763). An essay towards solving a problem in the doctrine of chances. By the late Rev. Mr. Bayes, communicated by Mr. Price, in a letter to John Canton, M. A. and F. R. S. *Philosophical Transactions of the Royal Society of London*, *53*, 370–418. https://doi.org/10.1098/rstl.1763.0053.

Beach, S. D., Ozernov-Palchik, O., May, S. C. et al. (2021). Neural decoding reveals concurrent phonemic and subphonemic representations of speech

across tasks. *Neurobiology of Language*, *2*(2), 254–79. https://doi.org/
10.1162/nol_a_00034.

Berthier, M. L., Starkstein, S. E., Leiguarda, R. et al. (1991). Transcortical aphasia: Importance of the nonspeech dominant hemisphere in language repetition. *Brain*, *114 (Pt 3)*, 1409–27. https://doi.org/10.1093/brain/114.3.1409.

Binder, J. R. (2015). The Wernicke area: Modern evidence and a reinterpretation. *Neurology*, *85*(24), 2170–5. https://doi.org/10.1212/wnl.0000000
000002219.

Binder, J. R., Desai, R. H., Graves, W. W., & Conant, L. L. (2009). Where is the semantic system? A critical review and meta-analysis of 120 functional neuroimaging studies. *Cerebral Cortex*, *19*(12), 2767–96. https://doi.org/
10.1093/cercor/bhp055.

Binder, J. R., Liebenthal, E., Possing, E. T., Medler, D. A., & Ward, B. D. (2004). Neural correlates of sensory and decision processes in auditory object identification. *Nature Neuroscience*, *7*(3), 295–301. https://doi.org/10.1038/
nn1198.

Boersma, P., & Weenink, D. (2023). Praat: doing phonetics by computer [Computer program]. www.praat.org/.

Bogen, J. E., & Bogen, G. M. (1976). Wernicke's region – where is it? *Annals of the New York Academy of Sciences*, *280*(1), 834–43. https://doi.org/10.1111/
j.1749-6632.1976.tb25546.x.

Bornkessel-Schlesewsky, I., & Schlesewsky, M. (2008). An alternative perspective on 'semantic P600' effects in language comprehension. *Brain Research Reviews*, *59*(1), 55–73. https://doi.org/10.1016/j.brainresrev.2008.05.003.

Bouillaud, J. (1825). Recherches cliniques propres à démontrer que la perte de la parole correspond à la lésion des lobules antérieures du cerveau, et à confirmer l'opinion de M. Gall sur le siège de l'organe du language articulé. *Archives Générales de Médecine*, *3*, 25–45.

Boyce, S., Browman, C. P., & Goldstein, L. (1987). Lexical organization and Welsh consonant mutations. *Journal of Memory and Language*, *26*(4), 419–52. https://doi.org/10.1016/0749-596X(87)90100-8.

Braga, R. M., Wilson, L. R., Sharp, D. J., Wise, R. J., & Leech, R. (2013). Separable networks for top-down attention to auditory non-spatial and visuospatial modalities. *Neuroimage*, *74*, 77–86. https://doi.org/10.1016/j.neuroimage.2013
.02.023.

Brass, M., & von Cramon, D. Y. (2004). Selection for cognitive control: A functional magnetic resonance imaging study on the selection of task-relevant information. *Journal of Neuroscience*, *24*(40), 8847–52. https://doi.org/10.1523/jneurosci.2513-04.2004.

Broadbent, D. E. (1954). The role of auditory localization in attention and memory span. *Journal of Experimental Psychology, 47*(3), 191–6. https://doi.org/10.1037/h0054182.

Broadbent, D. E. (1956). Successive responses to simultaneous stimuli. *Quarterly Journal of Experimental Psychology, 8*(4), 145–52. https://doi.org/10.1080/17470215608416814.

Broadbent, D. E., Ladefoged, P., & Lawrence, W. (1956). Vowel sounds and perceptual constancy. *Nature, 178*(4537), 815–6. https://doi.org/10.1038/178815b0.

Broca, P. P. (1861a). Nouvelle observation d'aphémie produite par une lésion de la moitié postérieure des deuxième et troisième circonvolutions frontales. *Bulletin de la Société Anatomique de Paris, 36*, 398–407.

Broca, P. P. (1861b). Perte de la parole, ramollissement chronique et destruction partielle du lobe antérieur gauche du cerveau. *Bulletin de la Société Anthropologique, 2*, 235–8.

Broca, P. P. (1861c). Remarques sur le siège de la faculté du langage articulé, suivies d'une observation d'aphémie (perte de la parole). *Bulletin de la Société Anatomique de Paris, 6*, 330–357.

Broca, P. P. (1865). Sur le siège de la faculté du langage articulé. *Bulletins de la Société d'anthropologie de Paris, 6*, 377–93.

Brodbeck, C., Hong, L. E., & Simon, J. Z. (2018). Rapid transformation from auditory to linguistic representations of continuous speech. *Current Biology, 28*(24), 3976–83. https://doi.org/10.1016/j.cub.2018.10.042.

Broderick, M. P., Anderson, A. J., & Lalor, E. C. (2019). Semantic context enhances the early auditory encoding of natural speech. *The Journal of Neuroscience, 39*(38), 7564. https://doi.org/10.1523/JNEUROSCI.0584-19.2019.

Brodmann, K. (1909). *Vergleichende Lokalisationslehre der Grosshirnrinde in ihren Prinzipien dargestellt auf Grund des Zellenbaues*. Leipzig: J.A. Barth.

Brouwer, H., Crocker, M. W., Venhuizen, N. J., & Hoeks, J. C. J. (2017). A neurocomputational model of the N400 and the P600 in language processing. *Cognitive Science, 41* (Suppl 6), 1318–52. https://doi.org/10.1111/cogs.12461.

Brugge, J. F., Volkov, I. O., Garell, P. C., Reale, R. A., & Howard, M. A. (2003). Functional connections between auditory cortex on Heschl's gyrus and on the lateral superior temporal gyrus in humans. *Journal of Neurophysiology, 90* (6), 3750–63. https://doi.org/10.1152/jn.00500.2003.

Brysbaert, M., Stevens, M., Mandera, P., & Keuleers, E. (2016). How many words do we know? Practical estimates of vocabulary size dependent on word definition, the degree of language input and the participant's age. *Frontiers in Psychology*, *7*, 1116. https://doi.org/10.3389/fpsyg.2016.01116.

Buchsbaum, B. R., Baldo, J., Okada, K. et al. (2011). Conduction aphasia, sensory-motor integration, and phonological short-term memory – an aggregate analysis of lesion and fMRI data. *Brain and Language*, *119*(3), 119–28. https://doi.org/10.1016/j.bandl.2010.12.001.

Carruthers, I. M., Laplagne, D. A., Jaegle, A. et al.(2015). Emergence of invariant representation of vocalizations in the auditory cortex. *Journal of Neurophysiology*, *114*(5), 2726–40. https://doi.org/10.1152/jn.00095.2015.

Casseday, J. H., Ehrlich, D., & Covey, E. (1994). Neural tuning for sound duration: Role of inhibitory mechanisms in the inferior colliculus. *Science*, *264*(5160), 847–50. https://doi.org/10.1126/science.8171341.

Casseday, J. H., Ehrlich, D., & Covey, E. (2000). Neural measurement of sound duration: Control by excitatory-inhibitory interactions in the inferior colliculus. *Journal of Neurophysiology*, *84*(3), 1475–87. https://doi.org/ 10.1152/jn.2000.84.3.1475.

Catani, M., Jones, D. K., & Ffytche, D. H. (2005). Perisylvian language networks of the human brain. *Annals of Neurology*, *57*(1), 8–16. https://doi .org/10.1002/ana.20319.

Caucheteux, C., Gramfort, A., & King, J.-R. (2023). Evidence of a predictive coding hierarchy in the human brain listening to speech. *Nature Human Behaviour*, *7*(3), 430–41. https://doi.org/10.1038/s41562-022-01516-2.

Cauchoix, M., Barragan-Jason, G., Serre, T., & Barbeau, E. J. (2014). The neural dynamics of face detection in the wild revealed by MVPA. *The Journal of Neuroscience*, *34*(3), 846. https://doi.org/10.1523/JNEUROSCI .3030-13.2014.

Chang, E. F., Rieger, J. W., Johnson, K. et al. (2010). Categorical speech representation in human superior temporal gyrus. *Nature Neuroscience*, *13* (11), 1428–32. https://doi.org/10.1038/nn.2641.

Chechik, G., & Nelken, I. (2012). Auditory abstraction from spectro-temporal features to coding auditory entities. *Proceedings of the National Academy of Sciences*, *109*(46), 18968–73. https://doi.org/10.1073/pnas.1111242109.

Cherry, E. C. (1953). Some experiments on the recognition of speech, with one and with two ears. *The Journal of the Acoustical Society of America*, *25*, 975–9. https://doi.org/10.1121/1.1907229.

Chi, T., Gao, Y., Guyton, M. C., Ru, P., & Shamma, S. (1999). Spectro-temporal modulation transfer functions and speech intelligibility. *The Journal of the Acoustical Society of America*, *106*(5), 2719–32. https://doi.org/10.1121/ 1.428100.

Chi, T., Ru, P., & Shamma, S. A. (2005). Multiresolution spectrotemporal analysis of complex sounds. *The Journal of the Acoustical Society of America, 118*(2), 887–906. https://doi.org/10.1121/1.1945807.

Chistovich, L. A. (1960). Классификация звуков речи при их быстром повторении [Classification of rapidly repeated speech sounds]. *Akusticheskii Zhurnal, 6*(3), 392–8.

Chomsky, N. (1957). *Syntactic Structures*. The Hague: Mouton.

Chomsky, N. (1965a). *Aspects of the Theory of Syntax*. Cambridge, MA: MIT Press.

Chomsky, N. (1965b). Persistent topics in linguistic theory. *Diogenes, 13*(51), 13–20. https://doi.org/10.1177/039219216501305102.

Chomsky, N., & Halle, M. (1968). *The Sound Pattern of English*. New York: Harper & Row.

Christianson, G. B., Sahani, M., & Linden, J. F. (2008). The consequences of response nonlinearities for interpretation of spectrotemporal receptive fields. *Journal of Neuroscience, 28*(2), 446–55. https://doi.org/10.1523/jneurosci.1775-07.2007.

Connolly, J. F., & Phillips, N. A. (1994). Event-related potential components reflect phonological and semantic processing of the terminal word of spoken sentences. *Journal of Cognitive Neuroscience, 6*(3), 256–66. https://doi.org/10.1162/jocn.1994.6.3.256.

Coomes, D. L., & Schofield, B. R. (2004). Projections from the auditory cortex to the superior olivary complex in guinea pigs. *European Journal of Neuroscience, 19*(8), 2188–200. https://doi.org/10.1111/j.0953-816X.2004.03317.x.

Cope, T. E., Sohoglu, E., Peterson, K. A. et al.(2023). Temporal lobe perceptual predictions for speech are instantiated in motor cortex and reconciled by inferior frontal cortex. *Cell Reports, 42*(5), 112422. https://doi.org/10.1016/j.celrep.2023.112422.

Cope, T. E., Sohoglu, E., Sedley, W. et al. (2017). Evidence for causal top-down frontal contributions to predictive processes in speech perception. *Nature Communications, 8*(1), 2154. https://doi.org/10.1038/s41467-017-01958-7.

Coulson, S., King, J. W., & Kutas, M. (1998). Expect the unexpected: Event-related brain response to morphosyntactic violations. *Language and Cognitive Processes, 13*(1), 21–58. https://doi.org/10.1080/016909698386582.

Cutler, A. (2012). *Native Listening: Language Experience and the Recognition of Spoken Words*. Massachusetts, MA: MIT Press.

Cutler, A., & Norris, D. (1988). The role of strong syllables in segmentation for lexical access. *Journal of Experimental Psychology-Human Perception and Performance, 14*(1), 113–21. https://doi.org/10.1037/0096-1523.14.1.113.

David, S. V., Mesgarani, N., Fritz, J. B., & Shamma, S. (2009). Rapid synaptic depression explains nonlinear modulation of spectro-temporal tuning in primary auditory cortex by natural stimuli. *The Journal of Neuroscience*, *29*(11), 3374–86. https://doi.org/10.1523/jneurosci.5249-08.2009.

Davis, M. H., & Gaskell, M. G. (2009). A complementary systems account of word learning: Neural and behavioural evidence. *Philosophical Transactions of the Royal Society B: Biological Sciences*, *364*(1536), 3773–800. https://doi.org/10.1098/rstb.2009.0111.

Dax, M. (1865). Lésions de la moitié gauche de l'encéphale coïncident avec l'oublie des signes de la pensée: Lu au Congrès méridional tenu à Montpellier en 1836, par le docteur Marc Dax. *Gazette Hebdomadaire de Médecine et de Chirurgie*, *17*, 259–60.

De Angelis, V., De Martino, F., Moerel, M. et al. (2018). Cortical processing of pitch: Model-based encoding and decoding of auditory fMRI responses to real-life sounds. *Neuroimage*, *180*(Pt A), 291–300. https://doi.org/10.1016/j.neuroimage.2017.11.020.

De Saussure, F. (1916). *Cours de linguistique générale* (C. Bailly, A. Séchehaye, & A. Riedlinger Eds.). Paris: Payot.

Dehaene-Lambertz, G., Pallier, C. et al.(2005). Neural correlates of switching from auditory to speech perception. *Neuroimage*, *24*(1), 21–33. https://doi.org/10.1016/j.neuroimage.2004.09.039.

Dejerine, J. (1895). *Anatomie des centres nerveux* (Vol. 1). Paris: Rueff et Compagnie.

DeLong, K. A., Urbach, T. P., & Kutas, M. (2005). Probabilistic word pre-activation during language comprehension inferred from electrical brain activity. *Nature Neuroscience*, *8*(8), 1117–21. https://doi.org/10.1038/nn1504.

Delorme, A. (2023). EEG is better left alone. *Scientific Reports*, *13*(1), 2372. https://doi.org/10.1038/s41598-023-27528-0.

DeWitt, I., & Rauschecker, J. P. (2012). Phoneme and word recognition in the auditory ventral stream. *Proceedings of the National Academy of Sciences*, *109*(8), E505–14. https://doi.org/10.1073/pnas.1113427109.

Diamond, I. T., Jones, E. G., & Powell, T. P. S. (1969). The projection of the auditory cortex upon the diencephalon and brain stem in the cat. *Brain Research*, *15*(2), 305–40. https://doi.org/10.1016/0006-8993(69)90160-7.

Diehl, R. L., Elman, J. L., & McCusker, S. B. (1978). Contrast effects on stop consonant identification. *Journal of Experimental Psychology: Human Perception and Performance*, *4*, 599–609. https://doi.org/10.1037/0096-1523.4.4.599.

Ding, N., & Simon, J. Z. (2009). Neural representations of complex temporal modulations in the human auditory cortex. *Journal of Neurophysiology, 102* (5), 2731–43. https://doi.org/10.1152/jn.00523.2009.

Dronkers, N. F., Plaisant, O., Iba-Zizen, M. T., & Cabanis, E. A. (2007). Paul Broca's historic cases: High resolution MR imaging of the brains of Leborgne and Lelong. *Brain, 130*(Pt 5), 1432–41. https://doi.org/10.1093/brain/awm042.

Durst-Andersen, P., & Bentsen, S. E. (2021). The word revisited: Introducing the CogSens Model to integrate semiotic, linguistic, and psychological perspectives. *Semiotica, 238,* 1–35. https://doi.org/10.1515/sem-2019-0041.

Ehrlich, D., Casseday, J. H., & Covey, E. (1997). Neural tuning to sound duration in the inferior colliculus of the big brown bat, Eptesicus fuscus. *Journal of Neurophysiology, 77*(5), 2360–72. https://doi.org/10.1152/jn.1997.77.5.2360.

Eldredge, D. H., & Miller, J. D. (1971). Physiology of hearing. *Annual Review of Physiology, 33*(1), 281–308. https://doi.org/10.1146/annurev.ph.33.030171.001433.

Elliott, L. L. (1962). Backward masking: Monotic and dichotic conditions. *The Journal of the Acoustical Society of America, 34*(8), 1108–15. https://doi.org/10.1121/1.1918253.

Elman, J. L. (2004). An alternative view of the mental lexicon. *Trends in Cognitive Sciences, 8*(7), 301–6. https://doi.org/10.1016/j.tics.2004.05.003.

Elman, J. L. (2009). On the meaning of words and dinosaur bones: Lexical knowledge without a lexicon. *Cognitive Science, 33*(4), 547–82. https://doi.org/10.1111/j.1551-6709.2009.01023.x.

Evans, N. (2000). Iwaidjan, a very un-Australian language family. *Linguistic Typology, 4*(1), 91–142.

Fant, G. (1970). *Acoustic Theory of Speech Production with Calculations Based on X-ray Studies of Russian Articulations* (2nd ed.). The Hague: Mouton.

Federmeier, K. D., & Kutas, M. (1999). A rose by any other name: Long-term memory structure and sentence processing. *Journal of Memory and Language, 41*(4), 469–95. https://doi.org/10.1006/jmla.1999.2660.

Federmeier, K. D., McLennan, D. B., De Ochoa, E., & Kutas, M. (2002). The impact of semantic memory organization and sentence context information on spoken language processing by younger and older adults: An ERP study. *Psychophysiology, 39*(5), 684–7. https://doi.org/10.1017.S004857720139203X.

Felix II, R. A., Gourévitch, B., Gómez-Álvarez, M. et al. (2017). Octopus cells in the posteroventral cochlear nucleus provide the main excitatory input to the superior paraolivary nucleus. *Frontiers in Neural Circuits, 11.*

Ferragamo, M. J., & Oertel, D. (2002). Octopus cells of the mammalian ventral cochlear nucleus sense the rate of depolarization. *Journal of Neurophysiology, 87*(5), 2262–70. https://doi.org/10.1152/jn.00587.2001.

Festen, J. M., & Plomp, R. (1990). Effects of fluctuating noise and interfering speech on the speech-reception threshold for impaired and normal hearing. *The Journal of the Acoustical Society of America, 88*(4), 1725–36. https://doi .org/10.1121/1.400247.

Fitzgibbons, P. J. (1984). Tracking a temporal gap in band-limited noise: Frequency and level effects. *Perception & Psychophysics, 35*(5), 446–50. https://doi.org/10.3758/BF03203921.

Fletcher, H. (1940). Auditory patterns. *Reviews of Modern Physics, 12*(1), 47–65. https://doi.org/10.1103/RevModPhys.12.47.

Fodor, J. A., & Bever, T. G. (1965). The psychological reality of linguistic segments. *Journal of Verbal Learning and Verbal Behavior, 4*(5), 414–20. https://doi.org/10.1016/S0022-5371(65)80081-0.

Formisano, E., De Martino, F., Bonte, M., & Goebel, R. (2008). 'Who' is saying 'what'? Brain-based decoding of human voice and speech. *Science, 322* (5903), 970–3.

Fox, P. T., Raichle, M. E., Mintun, M. A., & Dence, C. (1988). Nonoxidative glucose consumption during focal physiologic neural activity. *Science, 241* (4864), 462–4. https://doi.org/doi:10.1126/science.3260686.

Friederici, A. D. (2002). Towards a neural basis of auditory sentence processing. *Trends in Cognitive Sciences, 6*(2), 78–84. https://doi.org/ 10.1016/S1364-6613(00)01839-8.

Friston, K. (2005). A theory of cortical responses. *Philosophical Transactions of the Royal Society B: Biological Sciences, 360*(1456), 815–36. https://doi .org/10.1098/rstb.2005.1622.

Friston, K. (2018). Does predictive coding have a future? *Nature Neuroscience, 21*(8), 1019–21. https://doi.org/10.1038/s41593-018-0200-7.

Friston, K., Sajid, N., Quiroga-Martinez, D. R. et al.(2021). Active listening. *Hearing Research, 399,* 107998. https://doi.org/10.1016/j.heares.2020 .107998.

Fritz, J., Shamma, S., Elhilali, M., & Klein, D. (2003). Rapid task-related plasticity of spectrotemporal receptive fields in primary auditory cortex. *Nature Neuroscience, 6*(11), 1216–23. https://doi.org/10.1038/nn1141.

Froehlich, P., Collet, L., Chanal, J. M., & Morgon, A. (1990). Variability of the influence of a visual task on the active micromechanical properties of the cochlea. *Brain Research, 508*(2), 286–8. https://doi.org/10.1016/0006-8993 (90)90408-4.

Fry, D. B., Abramson, A. S., Eimas, P. D., & Liberman, A. M. (1962). The identification and discrimination of synthetic vowels. *Language and Speech*, *5*(4), 171–89. https://doi.org/10.1177/002383096200500401.

Gagnepain, P., Henson, R. N., & Davis, M. H. (2012). Temporal predictive codes for spoken words in auditory cortex. *Current Biology*, *22*(7), 615–21. https://doi.org/10.1016/j.cub.2012.02.015.

Galambos, R., & Davis, H. (1943). The response of single auditory-nerve fibers to acoustic stimulation. *Journal of Neurophysiology*, *6*(1), 39–57. https://doi.org/10.1152/jn.1943.6.1.39.

Galbraith, G. C., & Arroyo, C. (1993). Selective attention and brainstem frequency-following responses. *Biological Psychology*, *37*(1), 3–22. https://doi.org/10.1016/0301-0511(93)90024-3.

Gall, F. J., & Spurzheim, G. (1809). *Recherches sur le système nerveux en général et sur celui du cerveau en particulier.* Paris: F. Schoell.

Ganong, W. F. (1980). Phonetic categorization in auditory word perception. *Journal of Experimental Psychology: Human Perception and Performance, 6* (1), 110–25. https://doi.org/10.1037/0096-1523.6.1.110.

Garinis, A. C., Glattke, T., & Cone, B. K. (2011). The MOC reflex during active listening to speech. *Journal of Speech, Language, and Hearing Research, 54* (5), 1464–76. https://doi.org/10.1044/1092-4388(2011/10-0223).

Gaskell, M. G., & Marslen-Wilson, W. D. (1998). Mechanisms of phonological inference in speech perception. *Journal of Experimental Psychology: Human Perception and Performance, 24*, 380–96. https://doi.org/10.1037/0096-1523.24.2.380.

Geisler, W. S. (2011). Contributions of ideal observer theory to vision research. *Vision Research, 51*(7), 771–81. https://doi.org/10.1016/j.visres.2010.09.027.

Geisler, W. S., & Kersten, D. (2002). Illusions, perception and Bayes. *Nature Neuroscience, 5*(6), 508–10. https://doi.org/10.1038/nn0602-508.

Gelfand, J. R., & Bookheimer, S. Y. (2003). Dissociating neural mechanisms of temporal sequencing and processing phonemes. *Neuron, 38*(5), 831–42. https://doi.org/10.1016/s0896-6273(03)00285-x.

Geschwind, N. (1965a). Disconnexion syndromes in animals and man. I. *Brain, 88*(2), 237–94. https://doi.org/10.1093/brain/88.2.237.

Geschwind, N. (1965b). Disconnexion syndromes in animals and man. II. *Brain, 88*(3), 585–644. https://doi.org/10.1093/brain/88.3.585.

Geschwind, N. (1967). Wernicke's contribution to the study of aphasia. *Cortex, 3*(4), 449–63. https://doi.org/10.1016/S0010-9452(67)80030-3.

Giard, M.-H., Collet, L., Bouchet, P., & Pernier, J. (1994). Auditory selective attention in the human cochlea. *Brain Research, 633*(1), 353–6. https://doi.org/10.1016/0006-8993(94)91561-X.

Golding, N. L., Ferragamo, M. J., & Oertel, D. (1999). Role of intrinsic conductances underlying responses to transients in octopus cells of the cochlear nucleus. *Journal of Neuroscience, 19*(8), 2897. https://doi.org/10.1523/JNEUROSCI.19-08-02897.1999.

Goto, H. (1971). Auditory perception by normal Japanese adults of the sounds 'L' and 'R'. *Neuropsychologia, 9*(3), 317–23. https://doi.org/10.1016/0028-3932(71)90027-3.

Goucha, T., & Friederici, A. D. (2015). The language skeleton after dissecting meaning: A functional segregation within Broca's area. *Neuroimage, 114,* 294–302. https://doi.org/10.1016/j.neuroimage.2015.04.011.

Gow, D. W., Jr. (2012). The cortical organization of lexical knowledge: A dual lexicon model of spoken language processing. *Brain and Language, 121*(3), 273–88. https://doi.org/10.1016/j.bandl.2012.03.005.

Gow, D. W., Jr. , Segawa, J. A., Ahlfors, S. P., & Lin, F.-H. (2008). Lexical influences on speech perception: A Granger causality analysis of MEG and EEG source estimates. *Neuroimage, 43*(3), 614–23. https://doi.org/10.1016/j.neuroimage.2008.07.027.

Greenberg, S. (1980). *WPP, No. 52: Temporal Neural Coding of Pitch and Vowel Quality*: Department of Linguistics, UCLA.

Gregory, R. L. (1980). Perceptions as hypotheses. *Philosophical Transactions of the Royal Society of London. Series B, Biological Sciences, 290*(1038), 181–97.

Griffiths, T. D., & Hall, D. A. (2012). Mapping pitch representation in neural ensembles with fMRI. *The Journal of Neuroscience, 32*(39), 13343. https://doi.org/10.1523/JNEUROSCI.3813-12.2012.

Griffiths, T. D., & Warren, J. D. (2002). The planum temporale as a computational hub. *Trends in Neurosciences, 25*(7), 348–53. https://doi.org/10.1016/s0166-2236(02)02191-4.

Grootswagers, T., Wardle, S. G., & Carlson, T. A. (2017). Decoding dynamic brain patterns from evoked responses: A tutorial on multivariate pattern analysis applied to time series neuroimaging data. *Journal of Cognitive Neuroscience, 29*(4), 677–97. https://doi.org/10.1162/jocn_a_01068.

Grosjean, F. (1980). Spoken word recognition processes and the gating paradigm. *Perception & Psychophysics, 28*(4), 267–83.

Guinan, J. J., Jr. (2006). Olivocochlear efferents: Anatomy, physiology, function, and the measurement of efferent effects in humans. *Ear and Hearing, 27*(6), 589–7. https://doi.org/10.1097/01.aud.0000240507.83072.e7.

Gwilliams, L., King, J. R., Marantz, A., & Poeppel, D. (2022). Neural dynamics of phoneme sequences reveal position-invariant code for content and order.

Nature Communications, 13(1), 6606. https://doi.org/10.1038/s41467-022-34326-1.

Hall, J. W., & Peters, R. W. (1981). Pitch for nonsimultaneous successive harmonics in quiet and noise. *The Journal of the Acoustical Society of America, 69*(2), 509–13. https://doi.org/10.1121/1.385480.

Hasson, U., Skipper, J. I., Nusbaum, H. C., & Small, S. L. (2007). Abstract coding of audiovisual speech: Beyond sensory representation. *Neuron, 56*(6), 1116–26. https://doi.org/10.1016/j.neuron.2007.09.037.

Hawkins, S., & Nguyen, N. (2004). Influence of syllable-coda voicing on the acoustic properties of syllable-onset /l/ in English. *Journal of Phonetics, 32*(2), 199–231. https://doi.org/10.1016/S0095-4470(03)00031-7.

Hazan, V., & Rosen, S. (1991). Individual variability in the perception of cues to place contrasts in initial stops. *Perception & Psychophysics, 49*(2), 187–200. https://doi.org/10.3758/bf03205038.

Heid, S., & Hawkins, S. (2000). *An Acoustical Study of Long-Domain /r/ and /l/ Coarticulation*. Paper presented at the 5th Seminar on Speech Production: Models and Data.

Heinz, M. G., Colburn, H. S., & Carney, L. H. (2001). Evaluating auditory performance limits: I. one-parameter discrimination using a computational model for the auditory nerve. *Neural Computation, 13*(10), 2273–316. https://doi.org/10.1162/089976601750541804.

Held, H. (1893). Die centrale Gehörleitung. *Archiv für Anatomie und Physiologie: Anatomische Abteilung*, 201–48.

Helmholtz, H. (1867). *Handbuch der physiologischen Optik*. Leipzig: Leopold Voss.

Helmholtz, H. (1877/1895). *On the Sensations of Tone as a Physiological Basis for the Theory of Music* (A. J. Ellis, Trans.). London: Longmans, Green.

Helmholtz, H. (1878/1971). The facts of perception. In Russell Kahl (Ed.) *Selected writings of Hermann von Helmholtz* (1st ed.). Middletown: Wesleyan University Press, 698–726.

Hickok, G., & Poeppel, D. (2000). Towards a functional neuroanatomy of speech perception. *Trends in Cognitive Sciences, 4*(4), 131–8. https://doi.org/10.1016/s1364-6613(00)01463-7.

Hickok, G., & Poeppel, D. (2004). Dorsal and ventral streams: A framework for understanding aspects of the functional anatomy of language. *Cognition, 92*(1), 67–99. https://doi.org/10.1016/j.cognition.2003.10.011.

Hickok, G., & Poeppel, D. (2007). The cortical organization of speech processing. *Nature Reviews Neuroscience, 8*(5), 393–402. https://doi.org/10.1038/nrn2113.

Hilbert, D. (1912). *Grundzüge einer allgemeinen Theorie der linearen Integralgleichungen*. Leipzig: B. G. Teubner.

Hjelmslev, L. (1961 [1943]). *Prolegomena to a Theory of Language*. Madison: The University of Wisconsin Press.

Hockett, C. F. (1958). *A Course in Modern Linguistics*. New York: MacMillan.

Hohwy, J. (2020). New directions in predictive processing. *Mind & Language*, *35*(2), 209–23. https://doi.org/10.1111/mila.12281.

Holdgraf, C. R., de Heer, W., Pasley, B. et al.(2016). Rapid tuning shifts in human auditory cortex enhance speech intelligibility. *Nature Communications*, *7*(1), 13654. https://doi.org/10.1038/ncomms13654.

Holmes, V. M., & Forster, K. I. (1972). Click location and syntactic structure. *Perception & Psychophysics*, *12*(1), 9–15. https://doi.org/10.3758/BF03212836.

Holt, L. L., Lotto, A. J., & Kluender, K. R. (2000). Neighboring spectral content influences vowel identification. *The Journal of the Acoustical Society of America*, *108*(2), 710–22. https://doi.org/10.1121/1.429604.

Howard, M. A., Volkov, I. O., Mirsky, R. et al.(2000). Auditory cortex on the human posterior superior temporal gyrus. *Journal of Comparative Neurology*, *416*(1), 79–92. https://doi.org/10.1002/(sici)1096-9861(20000103)416:1<79::aid-cne6>3.0.co;2-2.

Howell, P., & Rosen, S. (1983). Production and perception of rise time in the voiceless affricate/fricative distinction. *The Journal of the Acoustical Society of America*, *73*(3), 976–84. https://doi.org/10.1121/1.389023.

Howes, D. (1957). On the relation between the intelligibility and frequency of occurrence of English words. *The Journal of the Acoustical Society of America*, *29*(2), 296–305. https://doi.org/10.1121/1.1908862.

Hudspeth, A. J. (1997). How hearing happens. *Neuron*, *19*(5), 947–50. https://doi.org/10.1016/s0896-6273(00)80385-2.

Huffman, R. F., & Henson, O. W., Jr. (1990). The descending auditory pathway and acousticomotor systems: Connections with the inferior colliculus. *Brain Research Reviews*, *15*(3), 295–323. https://doi.org/10.1016/0165-0173(90)90005-9.

Hullett, P. W., Hamilton, L. S., Mesgarani, N., Schreiner, C. E., & Chang, E. F. (2016). Human superior temporal gyrus organization of spectrotemporal modulation tuning derived from speech stimuli. *Journal of Neuroscience*, *36*(6), 2014–26. https://doi.org/10.1523/JNEUROSCI.1779-15.2016.

Huth, A. G., de Heer, W. A., Griffiths, T. L., Theunissen, F. E., & Gallant, J. L. (2016). Natural speech reveals the semantic maps that tile human cerebral cortex. *Nature*, *532*(7600), 453–8. https://doi.org/10.1038/nature17637.

Hutzler, F. (2014). Reverse inference is not a fallacy per se: Cognitive processes can be inferred from functional imaging data. *Neuroimage*, *84*, 1061–9. https://doi.org/10.1016/j.neuroimage.2012.12.075.

IEEE. (1969). IEEE Recommended practice for speech quality measurements. In *IEEE No 297–1969* (pp. 1–24).

Jakobson, R., Fant, G., & Halle, M. (1961). *Preliminaries to Speech Analysis: The Distinctive Features and Their Correlates*. Cambridge, MA: The MIT Press.

Jensen, M., Hyder, R., & Shtyrov, Y. (2019). MVPA analysis of intertrial phase coherence of neuromagnetic responses to words reliably classifies multiple levels of language processing in the brain. *eNeuro*, *6*(4). https://doi.org/10.1523/eneuro.0444-18.2019.

Jewett, D. L., & Williston, J. S. (1971). Auditory-evoked far fields averaged from the scalp of humans. *Brain*, *94*(4), 681–96. https://doi.org/10.1093/brain/94.4.681.

Jewett, D. L., Romano, M. N., & Williston, J. S. (1970). Human auditory evoked potentials: Possible brain stem components detected on the scalp. *Science*, *167*(3924), 1517–8. https://doi.org/10.1126/science.167.3924.1517.

Joanisse, M. F., Zevin, J. D., & McCandliss, B. D. (2007). Brain mechanisms implicated in the preattentive categorization of speech sounds revealed using FMRI and a short-interval habituation trial paradigm. *Cerebral Cortex*, *17*(9), 2084–93. https://doi.org/10.1093/cercor/bhl124.

Joris, P. X., & Yin, T. C. T. (1992). Responses to amplitude-modulated tones in the auditory nerve of the cat. *The Journal of the Acoustical Society of America*, *91*(1), 215–32. https://doi.org/10.1121/1.402757.

Joris, P. X., Schreiner, C. E., & Rees, A. (2004). Neural processing of amplitude-modulated sounds. *Physiological Reviews*, *84*(2), 541–77. https://doi.org/10.1152/physrev.00029.2003.

Jung, T. P., Makeig, S., Westerfield, M. et al. (2000). Removal of eye activity artifacts from visual event-related potentials in normal and clinical subjects. *Clinical Neurophysiology*, *111*(10), 1745–58. https://doi.org/10.1016/s1388-2457(00)00386-2.

Kabdebon, C., & Dehaene-Lambertz, G. (2019). Symbolic labeling in 5-month-old human infants. *Proceedings of the National Academy of Sciences*, *116*(12), 5805–10. https://doi.org/10.1073/pnas.1809144116.

Kang, S., Johnson, K., & Finley, G. (2016). Effects of native language on compensation for coarticulation. *Speech Communication*, *77*, 84–100. https://doi.org/10.1016/j.specom.2015.12.005.

Khalighinejad, B., Patel, P., Herrero, J. L. et al.(2021). Functional characterization of human Heschl's gyrus in response to natural speech. *Neuroimage*, *235*, 118003. https://doi.org/10.1016/j.neuroimage.2021.118003.

Kim, S.-G., Martino, F., & Overath, T. (2023). Linguistic modulation of the neural encoding of phonemes. *bioRxiv*, 2021.2007.2005.451175. https://doi.org/10.1101/2021.07.05.451175.

Kingston, J., Kawahara, S., Chambless, D. et al. (2014). Context effects as auditory contrast. *Attention, Perception & Psychophysics, 76,* 1437–64. https://doi.org/10.3758/s13414-013-0593-z.

Klatt, D., & Shattuck, S. R. (1974). *Perception of Brief Stimuli that Resemble Rapid Formant Transitions.* Paper presented at the 86th Meeting of the Acoustical Society of America, Los Angeles.

Knoeferle, P., Habets, B., Crocker, M. W., & Munte, T. F. (2008). Visual scenes trigger immediate syntactic reanalysis: Evidence from ERPs during situated spoken comprehension. *Cerebral Cortex, 18*(4), 789–95. https://doi.org/10.1093/cercor/bhm121.

Koumura, T., Terashima, H., & Furukawa, S. (2023). Human-like modulation sensitivity emerging through optimization to natural sound recognition. *The Journal of Neuroscience, 43*(21), 3876. https://doi.org/10.1523/JNEUROSCI.2002-22.2023.

Kowalski, N., Depireux, D. A., & Shamma, S. A. (1996). Analysis of dynamic spectra in ferret primary auditory cortex. I. Characteristics of single-unit responses to moving ripple spectra. *Journal of Neurophysiology, 76*(5), 3503–23. https://doi.org/10.1152/jn.1996.76.5.3503.

Kuhl, P. K. (1979). Speech perception in early infancy: Perceptual constancy for spectrally dissimilar vowel categories. *The Journal of the Acoustical Society of America, 66*(6), 1668–79. https://doi.org/10.1121/1.383639.

Kumar, S., Sedley, W., Nourski, K. V. et al. (2011). Predictive coding and pitch processing in the auditory cortex. *Journal of Cognitive Neuroscience, 23*(10), 3084–94. https://doi.org/10.1162/jocn_a_00021.

Kumar, S., Stephan, K. E., Warren, J. D., Friston, K. J., & Griffiths, T. D. (2007). Hierarchical processing of auditory objects in humans. *PLOS Computational Biology, 3*(6), e100. https://doi.org/10.1371/journal.pcbi.0030100.

Kuperberg, G. R., Brothers, T., & Wlotko, E. W. (2020). A tale of two positivities and the N400: Distinct neural signatures are evoked by confirmed and violated predictions at different levels of representation. *Journal of Cognitive Neuroscience, 32*(1), 12–35. https://doi.org/10.1162/jocn_a_01465.

Kuperberg, G. R., Sitnikova, T., Caplan, D., & Holcomb, P. J. (2003). Electrophysiological distinctions in processing conceptual relationships within simple sentences. *Cognitive Brain Research, 17*(1), 117–29. https://doi.org/10.1016/s0926-6410(03)00086-7.

Kutas, M., & Federmeier, K. D. (2011). Thirty years and counting: Finding meaning in the N400 component of the event-related brain potential (ERP). *Annual Review of Psychology, 62,* 621–47. https://doi.org/10.1146/annurev.psych.093008.131123.

Kutas, M., & Hillyard, S. A. (1980). Event-related brain potentials to semantically inappropriate and surprisingly large words. *Biological Psychology, 11* (2), 99–116. https://doi.org/10.1016/0301-0511(80)90046-0.

Ladefoged, P., & Broadbent, D. E. (1957). Information conveyed by vowels. *The Journal of the Acoustical Society of America, 29*(1), 98–104. https://doi.org/10.1121/1.1908694.

Lawrence, S. J. D., Formisano, E., Muckli, L., & de Lange, F. P. (2019). Laminar fMRI: Applications for cognitive neuroscience. *Neuroimage, 197,* 785–91. https://doi.org/10.1016/j.neuroimage.2017.07.004.

Lehiste, I. (1960). An acoustic-phonetic study of internal open juncture. *Phonetica, 5*(Suppl. 1), 5–54. https://doi.org/10.1159/000258062.

Leonard, M. K., & Chang, E. F. (2014). Dynamic speech representations in the human temporal lobe. *Trends in Cognitive Sciences, 18*(9), 472–9. https://doi.org/10.1016/j.tics.2014.05.001.

Leonard, M. K., Baud, M. O., Sjerps, M. J., & Chang, E. F. (2016). Perceptual restoration of masked speech in human cortex. *Nature Communications, 7*(1), 13619. https://doi.org/10.1038/ncomms13619.

Leonard, M. K., Bouchard, K. E., Tang, C., & Chang, E. F. (2015). Dynamic encoding of speech sequence probability in human temporal cortex. *The Journal of Neuroscience, 35*(18), 7203. https://doi.org/10.1523/JNEUROSCI.4100-14.2015.

Levinson, S. C., & Torreira, F. (2015). Timing in turn-taking and its implications for processing models of language. *Frontiers in Psychology, 6,* 1–17. https://doi.org/10.3389/fpsyg.2015.00731.

Liang, L., Lu, T., & Wang, X. (2002). Neural representations of sinusoidal amplitude and frequency modulations in the primary auditory cortex of awake primates. *Journal of Neurophysiology, 87*(5), 2237–61. https://doi.org/10.1152/jn.2002.87.5.2237.

Liberman, A. M., Cooper, F. S., Shankweiler, D. P., & Studdert-Kennedy, M. (1967). Perception of the speech code. *Psychological Review, 74*(6), 431–61. https://doi.org/10.1037/h0020279.

Liberman, A. M., Delattre, P., & Cooper, F. S. (1952). The role of selected stimulus-variables in the perception of the unvoiced stop consonants. *American Journal of Psychology, 65*(4), 497–516.

Liberman, A. M., Delattre, P. C., Cooper, F. S., & Gerstman, L. J. (1954). The role of consonant-vowel transitions in the perception of the stop and nasal consonants. *Psychological Monographs: General and Applied, 68*(8), 1–13. https://doi.org/10.1037/h0093673.

Liberman, A. M., Harris, K. S., Hoffman, H. S., & Griffith, B. C. (1957). The discrimination of speech sounds within and across phoneme boundaries.

Journal of Experimental Psychology, *54*, 358–68. https://doi.org/10.1037/h0044417.

Lichtheim, L. (1885). On aphasia. *Brain*, *7*, 433–84.

Liebenthal, E., Binder, J. R., Spitzer, S. M., Possing, E. T., & Medler, D. A. (2005). Neural Substrates of phonemic perception. *Cerebral Cortex*, *15*(10), 1621–31. https://doi.org/10.1093/cercor/bhi040.

Liégeois-Chauvel, C., Lorenzi, C., Trébuchon, A., Régis, J., & Chauvel, P. (2004). Temporal envelope processing in the human left and right auditory cortices. *Cerebral Cortex*, *14*(7), 731–40. https://doi.org/10.1093/cercor/bhh033.

Lindblom, B. (1990). Explaining phonetic variation: A sketch of the H&H theory. In W. J. Hardcastle & A. Marchal (Eds.), *Speech Production and Speech Modelling* (pp. 403–39). Dordrecht: Springer Netherlands.

Lindblom, B., & Studdert-Kennedy, M. (1967). On the role of formant transitions in vowel recognition. *The Journal of the Acoustical Society of America*, *42*(4), 830–43. https://doi.org/10.1121/1.1910655.

Lisker, L., & Abramson, A. S. (1964). A cross-language study of voicing in initial stops: Acoustical measurements. *Word*, *20*(3), 384–422.

Local, J., & Kelly, J. (1986). *Long Domain Resonance Patterns in English*. Paper presented at the IEE Conference on Speech Input/Output: Techniques and Applications.

Loizou, P. C., Dorman, M., & Tu, Z. M. (1999). On the number of channels needed to understand speech. *The Journal of the Acoustical Society of America*, *106*(4), 2097–103. https://doi.org/10.1121/1.427954.

Lotto, A. J., & Kluender, K. R. (1998). General contrast effects in speech perception: Effect of preceding liquid on stop consonant identification. *Perception & Psychophysics*, *60*(4), 602–19. https://doi.org/10.3758/bf03206049.

Luce, P. A., & Pisoni, D. B. (1998). Recognizing spoken words: The neighborhood activation model. *Ear and Hearing*, *19*(1), 1–36.

Luck, S. J. (2014). *An Introduction to the Event-Related Potential Technique* (2nd ed.). Cambridge, MA: MIT Press.

Luck, S. J., Woodman, G. F., & Vogel, E. K. (2000). Event-related potential studies of attention. *Trends in Cognitive Sciences*, *4*(11), 432–40. https://doi.org/10.1016/S1364-6613(00)01545-X.

Lulaci, T., Tronnier, M., Söderström, P., & Roll, M. (2022). *The Time Course of Onset CV Coarticulation*. Paper presented at the XXXIIIrd Swedish Phonetics Conference: Fonetik 2022, Stockholm, Sweden.

Luo, F., Wang, Q., Kashani, A., & Yan, J. (2008). Corticofugal modulation of initial sound processing in the brain. *The Journal of Neuroscience*, *28*(45), 11615–21. https://doi.org/10.1523/jneurosci.3972-08.2008.

MacGregor, L. J., Pulvermüller, F., van Casteren, M., & Shtyrov, Y. (2012). Ultra-rapid access to words in the brain. *Nature Communications*, *3*, 711. https://doi.org/10.1038/ncomms1715.

Mann, V. A. (1980). Influence of preceding liquid on stop-consonant perception. *Perception & Psychophysics*, *28*(5), 407–12. https://doi.org/10.3758/bf03204884.

Mann, V. A., & Repp, B. H. (1980). Influence of vocalic context on perception of the [ʃ]-[s] distinction. *Perception & Psychophysics*, *28*(3), 213–28. https://doi.org/10.3758/BF03204377.

Mann, V. A., & Repp, B. H. (1981). Influence of preceding fricative on stop consonant perception. *The Journal of the Acoustical Society of America*, *69* (2), 548–58. https://doi.org/10.1121/1.385483.

Manuel, S. (1999). Cross-language studies: Relating language-particular coarticulation patterns to other language-particular facts. In N. Hewlett & W. J. Hardcastle (Eds.), *Coarticulation: Theory, Data and Techniques* (pp. 179–98). Cambridge: Cambridge University Press.

Maris, E., & Oostenveld, R. (2007). Nonparametric statistical testing of EEG- and MEG-data. *Journal of Neuroscience Methods*, *164*(1), 177–90. https://doi.org/10.1016/j.jneumeth.2007.03.024.

Marslen-Wilson, W. D. (1973). Linguistic structure and speech shadowing at very short latencies. *Nature*, *244*(5417), 522–3.

Marslen-Wilson, W. D. (1975). Sentence perception as an interactive parallel process. *Science*, *189*(4198), 226–8.

Marslen-Wilson, W. D. (1985). Speech shadowing and speech comprehension. *Speech Communication*, *4*(1), 55–73. https://doi.org/10.1016/0167-6393(85)90036-6.

Marslen-Wilson, W. D., & Warren, P. (1994). Levels of perceptual representation and process in lexical access: Words, phonemes, and features. *Psychological Review*, *101*(4), 653–75. https://doi.org/10.1037/0033-295X.101.4.653.

Martinet, A. (1949). La double articulation linguistique. *Travaux du Cercle Linguistique de Copenhague*, *5*, 30–7.

Matsumoto, R., Nair, D. R., LaPresto, E. et al. (2004). Functional connectivity in the human language system: A cortico-cortical evoked potential study. *Brain*, *127*(10), 2316–30. https://doi.org/10.1093/brain/awh246.

McMurray, B., Tanenhaus, M. K., & Aslin, R. N. (2009). Within-category VOT affects recovery from 'lexical' garden paths: Evidence against phoneme-level inhibition. *Journal of Memory and Language*, *60*(1), 65–91. https://doi.org/10.1016/j.jml.2008.07.002.

McNealy, K., Mazziotta, J. C., & Dapretto, M. (2006). Cracking the language code: Neural mechanisms underlying speech parsing. *Journal of*

Neuroscience, 26(29), 7629–39. https://doi.org/10.1523/JNEUROSCI.5501-05.2006.

McQueen, J. M. (1998). Segmentation of continuous speech using phonotactics. *Journal of Memory and Language, 39*(1), 21–46. https://doi.org/10.1006/jmla.1998.2568.

McQueen, J. M., & Cox, E. (1995). *The Use of Phonotactic Constraints in the Segmentation of Dutch.* Paper presented at the Proceedings of the 4th European Conference on Speech Communication and Technology (Eurospeech 1995).

McQueen, J. M., Norris, D., & Cutler, A. (1994). Competition in spoken word recognition: Spotting words in other words. *Journal of Experimental Psychology: Learning, Memory, and Cognition, 20*, 621–38. https://doi.org/10.1037/0278-7393.20.3.621.

McQueen, J. M., Norris, D., & Cutler, A. (1999). Lexical influence in phonetic decision making: Evidence from subcategorical mismatches. *Journal of Experimental Psychology: Human Perception and Performance, 25*(5), 1363–1389. https://doi.org/10.1037/0096-1523.25.5.1363.

Mertes, I. B., Johnson, K. M., & Dinger, Z. A. (2019). Olivocochlear efferent contributions to speech-in-noise recognition across signal-to-noise ratios. *The Journal of the Acoustical Society of America, 145*(3), 1529–40, 1529. https://doi.org/10.1121/1.5094766.

Mesgarani, N., Cheung, C., Johnson, K., & Chang, E. F. (2014). Phonetic feature encoding in human superior temporal gyrus. *Science, 343*(6174), 1006–10. https://doi.org/10.1126/science.1245994.

Mesgarani, N., David, S. V., Fritz, J. B., & Shamma, S. A. (2008). Phoneme representation and classification in primary auditory cortex. *The Journal of the Acoustical Society of America, 123*(2), 899–909. https://doi.org/10.1121/1.2816572.

Mesgarani, N., David, S. V., Fritz, J. B., & Shamma, S. A. (2014). Mechanisms of noise robust representation of speech in primary auditory cortex. *Proceedings of the National Academy of Sciences, 111*(18), 6792–7. https://doi.org/10.1073/pnas.1318017111.

Meyer, A. S. (2023). Timing in conversation. *Journal of Cognition, 6*(1), 1–17. https://doi.org/10.5334/joc.268.

Meyer, D. E., & Schvaneveldt, R. W. (1971). Facilitation in recognizing pairs of words: Evidence of a dependence between retrieval operations. *Journal of Experimental Psychology, 90*(2), 227–34. https://doi.org/10.1037/h0031564.

Miller, G. A., Heise, G. A., & Lichten, W. (1951). The intelligibility of speech as a function of the context of the test materials. *Journal of Experimental Psychology, 41*(5), 329–35. https://doi.org/10.1037/h0062491.

Miller, J. L., & Liberman, A. M. (1979). Some effects of later-occurring information on the perception of stop consonant and semivowel. *Perception & Psychophysics, 25*(6), 457–65. https://doi.org/10.3758/bf03213823.

Miller, J. L., Green, K., & Schermer, T. M. (1984). A distinction between the effects of sentential speaking rate and semantic congruity on word identification. *Perception & Psychophysics, 36*(4), 329–37. https://doi.org/10.3758/BF03202785.

Miller, L. M., Escabí, M. A., Read, H. L., & Schreiner, C. E. (2001). Functional convergence of response properties in the auditory thalamocortical system. *Neuron, 32*(1), 151–60. https://doi.org/10.1016/s0896-6273(01)00445-7.

Milner, A. D., & Goodale, M. A. (1995). *The Visual Brain in Action.* New York: Oxford University Press.

Mitterer, H., & Blomert, L. (2003). Coping with phonological assimilation in speech perception: Evidence for early compensation. *Perception & Psychophysics, 65*(6), 956–69. https://doi.org/10.3758/BF03194826.

Mitterer, H., Csépe, V., & Blomert, L. (2006). The role of perceptual integration in the recognition of assimilated word forms. *Quarterly Journal of Experimental Psychology, 59*(8), 1395–424. https://doi.org/10.1080/17470210500198726.

Miyawaki, K., Jenkins, J. J., Strange, W. et al. (1975). An effect of linguistic experience: The discrimination of [r] and [l] by native speakers of Japanese and English. *Perception & Psychophysics, 18*(5), 331–40. https://doi.org/10.3758/BF03211209.

Mohr, J. P., Pessin, M. S., Finkelstein, S. et al.(1978). Broca aphasia: Pathologic and clinical. *Neurology, 28*(4), 311–24. https://doi.org/10.1212/wnl.28.4.311.

Moore, B. C., Glasberg, B. R., & Baer, T. (1997). A model for the prediction of thresholds, loudness, and partial loudness. *Journal of the Audio Engineering Society, 45*(4), 224–40.

Morosan, P., Rademacher, J., Schleicher, A. et al. (2001). Human primary auditory cortex: Cytoarchitectonic subdivisions and mapping into a spatial reference system. *Neuroimage, 13*(4), 684–701. https://doi.org/10.1006/nimg.2000.0715.

Morosan, P., Schleicher, A., Amunts, K., & Zilles, K. (2005). Multimodal architectonic mapping of human superior temporal gyrus. *Anatomy and Embryology, 210*(5–6), 401–6. https://doi.org/10.1007/s00429-005-0029-1.

Moushegian, G., Rupert, A. L., & Stillman, R. D. (1973). Laboratory note: Scalp-recorded early responses in man to frequencies in the speech range. *Electroencephalography and Clinical Neurophysiology, 35*(6), 665–7. https://doi.org/10.1016/0013-4694(73)90223-x.

Myers, E. B., Blumstein, S. E., Walsh, E., & Eliassen, J. (2009). Inferior frontal regions underlie the perception of phonetic category invariance. *Psychological Science, 20*(7), 895–903. https://doi.org/10.1111/j.1467-9280.2009.02380.x.

Näätänen, R. (1995). The mismatch negativity: A powerful tool for cognitive neuroscience. *Ear and Hearing, 16*(1), 6–18.

Näätänen, R., & Picton, T. W. (1987). The N1 wave of the human electric and magnetic response to sound: A review and an analysis of the component structure. *Psychophysiology, 24*(4), 375–425. https://doi.org/10.1111/j.1469-8986.1987.tb00311.x.

Näätänen, R., Gaillard, A. W. K., & Mäntysalo, S. (1978). Early selective-attention effect on evoked potential reinterpreted. *Acta Psychologica, 42*(4), 313–29. https://doi.org/10.1016/0001-6918(78)90006-9.

Näätänen, R., Lehtokoski, A., Lennes, M. et al.(1997). Language-specific phoneme representations revealed by electric and magnetic brain responses. *Nature, 385*(6615), 432–4. https://doi.org/10.1038/385432a0.

Nelken, I. (2004). Processing of complex stimuli and natural scenes in the auditory cortex. *Current Opinion in Neurobiology, 14*(4), 474–80. https://doi.org/10.1016/j.conb.2004.06.005.

Nelken, I. (2008). Processing of complex sounds in the auditory system. *Current Opinion in Neurobiology, 18*(4), 413–7. https://doi.org/10.1016/j.conb.2008.08.014.

Nelken, I., Fishbach, A., Las, L., Ulanovsky, N., & Farkas, D. (2003). Primary auditory cortex of cats: feature detection or something else? *Biological Cybernetics, 89*(5), 397–406. https://doi.org/10.1007/s00422-003-0445-3.

Newman, A. J., Ullman, M. T., Pancheva, R., Waligura, D. L., & Neville, H. J. (2007). An ERP study of regular and irregular English past tense inflection. *Neuroimage, 34*(1), 435–45. https://doi.org/10.1016/j.neuroimage.2006.09.007.

Newman, R. L., & Connolly, J. F. (2009). Electrophysiological markers of pre-lexical speech processing: Evidence for bottom-up and top-down effects on spoken word processing. *Biological Psychology, 80*(1), 114–21. https://doi.org/10.1016/j.biopsycho.2008.04.008.

Newman, R. L., Connolly, J. F., Service, E., & McIvor, K. (2003). Influence of phonological expectations during a phoneme deletion task: Evidence from event-related brain potentials. *Psychophysiology, 40*(4), 640–7. https://doi.org/10.1111/1469-8986.00065.

Newman, R. S., Clouse, S. A., & Burnham, J. L. (2001). The perceptual consequences of within-talker variability in fricative production. *The*

Journal of the Acoustical Society of America, 109(3), 1181–96. https://doi
.org/10.1121/1.1348009.

Norris, D., & Cutler, A. (2021). More why, less how: What we need from
models of cognition. *Cognition, 213,* 104688. https://doi.org/10.1016/
j.cognition.2021.104688.

Norris, D., & McQueen, J. M. (2008). Shortlist B: A Bayesian model of
continuous speech recognition. *Psychological Review, 115*(2), 357–95.
https://doi.org/10.1037/0033-295X.115.2.357.

Norris, D., McQueen, J. M., & Cutler, A. (1995). Competition and segmentation
in spoken-word recognition. *Journal of Experimental Psychology: Learning
Memory and Cognition, 21*(5), 1209–28. https://doi.org/10.1037/0278-
7393.21.5.1209.

Norris, D., McQueen, J. M., & Cutler, A. (2003). Perceptual learning in speech.
Cognitive Psychology, 47, 204–38. https://doi.org/10.1016/S0010-0285(03)
00006-9.

Norris, D., McQueen, J. M., & Cutler, A. (2016). Prediction, Bayesian inference
and feedback in speech recognition. *Language, Cognition and Neuroscience,
31*(1), 4–18. https://doi.org/10.1080/23273798.2015.1081703.

Nour Eddine, S., Brothers, T., & Kuperberg, G. R. (2022). The N400 in silico:
A review of computational models. In K. D. Federmeier (Ed.), *Psychology of
Learning and Motivation* (Vol. 76, pp. 123–206). Cambridge, MA: Academic
Press.

Numssen, O., Bzdok, D., & Hartwigsen, G. (2021). Functional specialization
within the inferior parietal lobes across cognitive domains. *Elife, 10,* 1–25.
https://doi.org/10.7554/eLife.63591.

O'Neill, J. J. (1957). Recognition of intelligibility test materials in context and
isolation. *Journal of Speech and Hearing Disorders, 22*(1), 87–90. https://
doi.org/10.1044/jshd.2201.87.

Obleser, J., Zimmermann, J., Van Meter, J., & Rauschecker, J. P. (2007). Multiple
stages of auditory speech perception reflected in event-related FMRI. *Cerebral
Cortex, 17*(10), 2251–7. https://doi.org/10.1093/cercor/bhl133.

Oertel, D., Bal, R., Gardner, S. M., Smith, P. H., & Joris, P. X. (2000). Detection
of synchrony in the activity of auditory nerve fibers by octopus cells of the
mammalian cochlear nucleus. *Proceedings of the National Academy of
Sciences, 97*(22), 11773–9. https://doi.org/10.1073/pnas.97.22.11773.

Ogawa, S., & Lee, T. M. (1990). Magnetic resonance imaging of blood vessels
at high fields: In vivo and in vitro measurements and image simulation.
Magnetic Resonance in Medicine, 16(1), 9–18.

Ogawa, S., Lee, T. M., Kay, A. R., & Tank, D. W. (1990). Brain magnetic
resonance imaging with contrast dependent on blood oxygenation.

Proceedings of the National Academy of Sciences, 87(24), 9868–72. https:// doi.org/10.1073/pnas.87.24.9868.

Ogawa, S., Lee, T. M., Nayak, A. S., & Glynn, P. (1990). Oxygenation-sensitive contrast in magnetic resonance image of rodent brain at high magnetic fields. *Magnetic Resonance in Medicine, 14*(1), 68–78.

Öhman, S. E. (1966). Coarticulation in VCV utterances: Spectrographic measurements. *The Journal of the Acoustical Society of America, 39*(1), 151–68. https://doi.org/10.1121/1.1909864.

Okada, K., & Hickok, G. (2006). Identification of lexical-phonological networks in the superior temporal sulcus using functional magnetic resonance imaging. *Neuroreport, 17*(12), 1293–6. https://doi.org/10.1097/01 .wnr.0000233091.82536.b2.

Osterhout, L., & Holcomb, P. J. (1992). Event-related brain potentials elicited by syntactic anomaly. *Journal of Memory and Language, 31*(6), 785–806. https://doi.org/10.1016/0749-596x(92)90039-Z.

Osterhout, L., & Mobley, L. A. (1995). Event-related brain potentials elicited by failure to agree. *Journal of Memory and Language, 34*(6), 739–73. https:// doi.org/10.1006/jmla.1995.1033.

Osterhout, L., Poliakov, A., Inoue, K. et al.(2008). Second-language learning and changes in the brain. *Journal of Neurolinguistics, 21*(6), 509–21. https:// doi.org/10.1016/j.jneuroling.2008.01.001.

Overath, T., & Lee, J. C. (2017). *The Neural Processing of Phonemes is Shaped by Linguistic Analysis*. Paper presented at the International Symposium on Auditory and Audiological Research.

Overath, T., McDermott, J. H., Zarate, J. M., & Poeppel, D. (2015). The cortical analysis of speech-specific temporal structure revealed by responses to sound quilts. *Nature Neuroscience, 18*(6), 903–11. https://doi.org/10.1038/nn.4021.

Pandya, D., Petrides, M., Cipolloni, P. B., & Petrides, M. (2015). *Cerebral Cortex: Architecture, Connections, and the Dual Origin Concept*. New York: Oxford University Press.

Pasley, B. N., David, S. V., Mesgarani, N. et al.(2012). Reconstructing speech from human auditory cortex. *PLOS Biology, 10*(1), e1001251. https://doi.org/ 10.1371/journal.pbio.1001251.

Pastore, R. E., & Farrington, S. M. (1996). Measuring the difference limen for identification of order of onset for complex auditory stimuli. *Perception & Psychophysics, 58*(4), 510–26. https://doi.org/10.3758/BF03213087.

Perez, C. A., Engineer, C. T., Jakkamsetti, V. et al.(2013). Different timescales for the neural coding of consonant and vowel sounds. *Cerebral Cortex, 23*(3), 670–83. https://doi.org/10.1093/cercor/bhs045.

Pernet, C. R., Latinus, M., Nichols, T. E., & Rousselet, G. A. (2015). Cluster-based computational methods for mass univariate analyses of event-related brain potentials/fields: A simulation study. *Journal of Neuroscience Methods*, *250*, 85–93. https://doi.org/10.1016/j.jneumeth.2014.08.003.

Petersen, S. E., & Posner, M. I. (2012). The attention system of the human brain: 20 years after. *Annual Review of Neuroscience*, *35*, 73–89. https://doi.org/10.1146/annurev-neuro-062111-150525.

Peterson, G. E., & Barney, H. L. (1952). Control methods used in a study of the vowels. *The Journal of the Acoustical Society of America*, *24*(2), 175–84. https://doi.org/10.1121/1.1906875.

Phillips, D. P., Hall, S. E., & Boehnke, S. E. (2002). Central auditory onset responses, and temporal asymmetries in auditory perception. *Hearing Research*, *167*(1–2), 192–205. https://doi.org/10.1016/s0378-5955(02)00393-3.

Picinbono, B. (1997). On instantaneous amplitude and phase of signals. *IEEE Transactions on Signal Processing*, *45*(3), 552–60. https://doi.org/10.1109/78.558469.

Picton, T. W., & Hillyard, S. A. (1972). Cephalic skin potentials in electroencephalography. *Electroencephalography and Clinical Neurophysiology*, *33*(4), 419–24. https://doi.org/10.1016/0013-4694(72)90122-8.

Pitt, M. A., & McQueen, J. M. (1998). Is compensation for coarticulation mediated by the lexicon? *Journal of Memory and Language*, *39*(3), 347–70. https://doi.org/10.1006/jmla.1998.2571.

Poeppel, D. (2001). Pure word deafness and the bilateral processing of the speech code. *Cognitive Science*, *25*(5), 679–93. https://doi.org/10.1207/s15516709cog2505_3.

Poeppel, D. (2003). The analysis of speech in different temporal integration windows: Cerebral lateralization as 'asymmetric sampling in time'. *Speech Communication*, *41*(1), 245–55. https://doi.org/10.1016/S0167-6393(02)00107-3.

Poeppel, D., & Hickok, G. (2004). Towards a new functional anatomy of language. *Cognition*, *92*(1–2), 1–12. https://doi.org/10.1016/j.cognition.2003.11.001.

Poldrack, R. A. (2006). Can cognitive processes be inferred from neuroimaging data? *Trends in Cognitive Sciences*, *10*(2), 59–63. https://doi.org/10.1016/j.tics.2005.12.004.

Pollack, I., Rubenstein, H., & Decker, L. (1960). Analysis of incorrect responses to an unknown message set. *The Journal of the Acoustical Society of America*, *32*(4), 454–7. https://doi.org/10.1121/1.1908097.

Portfors, C. V., & Sinex, D. G. (2005). Coding of communication sounds in the inferior colliculus. In J. A. Winer & C. E. Schreiner (Eds.), *The Inferior Colliculus*, New York, NY: Springer, 411–25.

Pratt, H. (2011). Sensory ERP components. In E. S. Kappenman & S. J. Luck (Eds.), *The Oxford Handbook of Event-Related Potential Components*, New York, NY: Oxford University Press, 81–14.

Price, C. N., & Bidelman, G. M. (2021). Attention reinforces human cortico-fugal system to aid speech perception in noise. *Neuroimage, 235*, 118014. https://doi.org/10.1016/j.neuroimage.2021.118014.

Pulvermüller, F., & Shtyrov, Y. (2008). Spatiotemporal signatures of large-scale synfire chains for speech processing as revealed by MEG. *Cerebral Cortex, 19*(1), 79–88. https://doi.org/10.1093/cercor/bhn060.

Pulvermüller, F., Shtyrov, Y., & Ilmoniemi, R. (2003). Spatiotemporal dynamics of neural language processing: An MEG study using minimum-norm current estimates. *Neuroimage, 20*(2), 1020–5. https://doi.org/10.1016/S1053-8119(03)00356-2.

Qin, M. K., & Oxenham, A. J. (2003). Effects of simulated cochlear-implant processing on speech reception in fluctuating maskers. *The Journal of the Acoustical Society of America, 114*(1), 446–54. https://doi.org/10.1121/1.1579009.

Raizada, R. D., & Poldrack, R. A. (2007). Selective amplification of stimulus differences during categorical processing of speech. *Neuron, 56*(4), 726–40. https://doi.org/10.1016/j.neuron.2007.11.001.

Rao, R. P., & Ballard, D. H. (1999). Predictive coding in the visual cortex: A functional interpretation of some extra-classical receptive-field effects. *Nature Neuroscience, 2*(1), 79–87. https://doi.org/10.1038/4580.

Rauschecker, J. P. (1998). Cortical processing of complex sounds. *Current Opinion in Neurobiology, 8*(4), 516–21. https://doi.org/10.1016/S0959-4388(98)80040-8.

Rauschecker, J. P., & Scott, S. K. (2009). Maps and streams in the auditory cortex: Nonhuman primates illuminate human speech processing. *Nature Neuroscience, 12*(6), 718–24. https://doi.org/10.1038/nn.2331.

Rees, A., & Møller, A. R. (1987). Stimulus properties influencing the responses of inferior colliculus neurons to amplitude-modulated sounds. *Hearing Research, 27*(2), 129–43. https://doi.org/10.1016/0378-5955(87)90014-1.

Rees, A., & Palmer, A. R. (1989). Neuronal responses to amplitude-modulated and pure-tone stimuli in the guinea pig inferior colliculus, and their modification by broadband noise. *The Journal of the Acoustical Society of America, 85*(5), 1978–94. https://doi.org/10.1121/1.397851.

Remez, R. E., Ferro, D. F., Dubowski, K. R. et al. (2010). Is desynchrony tolerance adaptable in the perceptual organization of speech? *Attention, Perception, & Psychophysics*, *72*(8), 2054–8. https://doi.org/10.3758/BF03196682.

Remez, R. E., Ferro, D. F., Wissig, S. C., & Landau, C. A. (2008). Asynchrony tolerance in the perceptual organization of speech. *Psychonomic Bulletin & Review*, *15*(4), 861–5. https://doi.org/10.3758/PBR.15.4.861.

Remez, R. E., Rubin, P. E., Pisoni, D. B., & Carrell, T. D. (1981). Speech perception without traditional speech cues. *Science*, *212*(4497), 947–50. https://doi.org/10.1126/science.7233191.

Repp, B. H. (1978). Perceptual integration and differentiation of spectral cues for intervocalic stop consonants. *Perception & Psychophysics*, *24*(5), 471–485. doi:10.3758/BF03199746

Repp, B. H. (1988). Integration and segregation in speech perception. *Language and Speech*, *31*(3), 239–71. https://doi.org/10.1177/002383098803100302.

Repp, B. H., & Liberman, A. M. (1987). Phonetic category boundaries are flexible. In S. R. Harnad (Ed.), *Categorical Perception: The Groundwork of Cognition* (pp. 89–112). New York: Cambridge University Press.

Repp, B. H., Liberman, A. M., Eccardt, T., & Pesetsky, D. (1978). Perceptual integration of acoustic cues for stop, fricative, and affricate manner. *Journal of Experimental Psychology: Human Perception and Performance*, *4*(4), 621–37. https://doi.org/10.1037//0096-1523.4.4.621.

Rhode, W. S. (1994). Temporal coding of 200% amplitude modulated signals in the ventral cochlear nucleus of cat. *Hearing Research*, *77*(1–2), 43–68. https://doi.org/10.1016/0378-5955(94)90252-6.

Rhode, W. S. (1998). Neural encoding of single-formant stimuli in the ventral cochlear nucleus of the chinchilla. *Hearing Research*, *117*(1), 39–56. https://doi.org/10.1016/S0378-5955(98)00002-1.

Rhode, W. S., & Greenberg, S. (1994). Encoding of amplitude modulation in the cochlear nucleus of the cat. *Journal of Neurophysiology*, *71*(5), 1797–825. https://doi.org/10.1152/jn.1994.71.5.1797.

Righi, G., Blumstein, S. E., Mertus, J., & Worden, M. S. (2010). Neural systems underlying lexical competition: An eye tracking and fMRI study. *Journal of Cognitive Neuroscience*, *22*(2), 213–24. https://doi.org/10.1162/jocn.2009.21200.

Rodríguez, F. A., Read, H. L., & Escabí, M. A. (2010). Spectral and temporal modulation tradeoff in the inferior colliculus. *Journal of Neurophysiology*, *103*(2), 887–903. https://doi.org/10.1152/jn.00813.2009.

Roll, M., Söderström, P., Frid, J., Mannfolk, P., & Horne, M. (2017). Forehearing words: Pre-activation of word endings at word onset.

Neuroscience Letters, 658, 57–61. https://doi.org/10.1016/j.neulet.2017
.08.030.

Roll, M., Söderström, P., Hjortdal, A., & Horne, M. (2023). Pre-activation
negativity (PrAN): A neural index of predictive strength of phonological
cues. *Laboratory Phonology, 14*(1), 1–33. https://doi.org/10.16995/
labphon.6438.

Roll, M., Söderström, P., Mannfolk, P. et al.(2015). Word tones cueing morphosyntactic structure: Neuroanatomical substrates and activation time-course
assessed by EEG and fMRI. *Brain and Language, 150,* 14–21. https://doi
.org/10.1016/j.bandl.2015.07.009.

Romani, G. L., Williamson, S. J., & Kaufman, L. (1982). Tonotopic organization of the human auditory cortex. *Science, 216*(4552), 1339–40. https://doi
.org/10.1126/science.7079770.

Rose, J. E., Brugge, J. F., Anderson, D. J., & Hind, J. E. (1967). Phase-locked
response to low-frequency tones in single auditory nerve fibers of the squirrel
monkey. *Journal of Neurophysiology, 30*(4), 769–93. https://doi.org/10.1152/
jn.1967.30.4.769.

Rosen, S. (1992). Temporal information in speech: Acoustic, auditory and
linguistic aspects. *Philosophical Transactions of the Royal Society B:
Biological Sciences, 336*(1278), 367–73. https://doi.org/10.1098/
rstb.1992.0070.

Rouiller, E. M. (1997). Functional organization of the auditory pathways. In
G. R. Ehret (Ed.), *The Central Auditory System.* Oxford: Oxford University
Press.

Rubenstein, H., Garfield, L., & Millikan, J. A. (1970). Homographic entries in
the internal lexicon. *Journal of Verbal Learning and Verbal Behavior, 9*(5),
487–94. https://doi.org/10.1016/S0022-5371(70)80091-3.

Rupp, A., Uppenkamp, S., Gutschalk, A. et al. (2002). The representation of
peripheral neural activity in the middle-latency evoked field of primary
auditory cortex in humans. *Hearing Research, 174*(1), 19–31. https://doi
.org/10.1016/S0378-5955(02)00614-7.

Russo, N., Nicol, T., Musacchia, G., & Kraus, N. (2004). Brainstem responses
to speech syllables. *Clinical Neurophysiology, 115*(9), 2021–30. https://doi
.org/10.1016/j.clinph.2004.04.003.

Sacks, H., Schegloff, E. A., & Jefferson, G. (1974). A simplest systematics for
the organization of turn-taking for conversation. *Language, 50*(4), 696–735.
https://doi.org/10.2307/412243.

Samuel, A. G. (1981a). Phonemic restoration: Insights from a new methodology.
Journal of Experimental Psychology: General, 110(4), 474–94. https://doi.org/
10.1037//0096-3445.110.4.474.

Samuel, A. G. (1981b). The role of bottom-up confirmation in the phonemic restoration illusion. *Journal of Experimental Psychology: Human Perception and Performance*, *7*(5), 1124–31. https://doi.org/10.1037/0096-1523.7.5.1124.

Santoro, R., Moerel, M., De Martino, F. et al.(2014). Encoding of natural sounds at multiple spectral and temporal resolutions in the human auditory cortex. *PLOS Computational Biology*, *10*(1), e1003412. https://doi.org/10.1371/jour nal.pcbi.1003412.

Sassenhagen, J., & Draschkow, D. (2019). Cluster-based permutation tests of MEG/EEG data do not establish significance of effect latency or location. *Psychophysiology*, *56*(6), e13335. https://doi.org/10.1111/psyp.13335.

Sassenhagen, J., Schlesewsky, M., & Bornkessel-Schlesewsky, I. (2014). The P600-as-P3 hypothesis revisited: Single-trial analyses reveal that the late EEG positivity following linguistically deviant material is reaction time aligned. *Brain and Language*, *137*, 29–39. https://doi.org/10.1016/j.bandl .2014.07.010.

Savin, H. B. (1963). Word-Frequency Effect and Errors in the Perception of Speech. *The Journal of the Acoustical Society of America*, *35*(2), 200–6. https://doi.org/10.1121/1.1918432.

Sayles, M., Stasiak, A., & Winter, I. M. (2016). Neural segregation of concurrent speech: Effects of background noise and reverberation on auditory scene analysis in the ventral cochlear nucleus. *Advances in Experimental Medicine and Biology*, *894*, 389–97. https://doi.org/10.1007/978-3-319-25474-6_41.

Scheich, H., Brechmann, A., Brosch, M., Budinger, E., & Ohl, F. W. (2007). The cognitive auditory cortex: Task-specificity of stimulus representations. *Hearing Research*, *229*(1–2), 213–24. https://doi.org/10.1016/j.heares .2007.01.025.

Schofield, B. R., & Coomes, D. L. (2006). Pathways from auditory cortex to the cochlear nucleus in guinea pigs. *Hearing Research*, *216–217*, 81–9. https:// doi.org/10.1016/j.heares.2006.01.004.

Schönwiesner, M., Novitski, N., Pakarinen, S. et al. (2007). Heschl's gyrus, posterior superior temporal gyrus, and mid-ventrolateral prefrontal cortex have different roles in the detection of acoustic changes. *Journal of Neurophysiology*, *97*(3), 2075–82. https://doi.org/10.1152/jn.01083.2006.

Schreiber, K. E., & McMurray, B. (2019). Listeners can anticipate future segments before they identify the current one. *Attention, Perception, & Psychophysics*, *81*(4), 1147–66. https://doi.org/10.3758/s13414-019-01712-9.

Schreiner, C. E., & Urbas, J. V. (1986). Representation of amplitude modulation in the auditory cortex of the cat. I. The anterior auditory field (AAF). *Hearing Research*, *21*(3), 227–41. https://doi.org/10.1016/0378-5955(86)90221-2.

Schröger, E. (1997). On the detection of auditory deviations: A pre-attentive activation model. *Psychophysiology*, *34*(3), 245–57. https://doi.org/10.1111/j.1469-8986.1997.tb02395.x.

Schuller, G. (1979). Coding of small sinusoidal frequency and amplitude modulations in the inferior colliculus of 'CF-FM' bat, Rhinolophus ferrumequinum. *Experimental Brain Research*, *34*(1), 117–32. https://doi.org/10.1007/bf00238345.

Scott, S. K., & Johnsrude, I. S. (2003). The neuroanatomical and functional organization of speech perception. *Trends in Neurosciences*, *26*(2), 100–7. https://doi.org/10.1016/S0166-2236(02)00037-1.

Shamma, S. (2001). On the role of space and time in auditory processing. *Trends in Cognitive Sciences*, *5*(8), 340–8. https://doi.org/10.1016/s1364-6613(00)01704-6.

Shamma, S., & Lorenzi, C. (2013). On the balance of envelope and temporal fine structure in the encoding of speech in the early auditory system. *The Journal of the Acoustical Society of America*, *133*(5), 2818–33. https://doi.org/10.1121/1.4795783.

Shannon, R. V., Zeng, F.-G., & Wygonski, J. (1998). Speech recognition with altered spectral distribution of envelope cues. *The Journal of the Acoustical Society of America*, *104*(4), 2467–76. https://doi.org/10.1121/1.423774.

Shannon, R. V., Zeng, F. G., Kamath, V., Wygonski, J., & Ekelid, M. (1995). Speech recognition with primarily temporal cues. *Science*, *270*(5234), 303–4. https://doi.org/10.1126/science.270.5234.303.

Sharpee, T. O., Atencio, C. A., & Schreiner, C. E. (2011). Hierarchical representations in the auditory cortex. *Current Opinion in Neurobiology*, *21*(5), 761–7. https://doi.org/10.1016/j.conb.2011.05.027.

Shtyrov, Y., & Lenzen, M. (2017). First-pass neocortical processing of spoken language takes only 30 msec: Electrophysiological evidence. *Cognitive Neuroscience*, *8*(1), 24–38. https://doi.org/10.1080/17588928.2016.1156663.

Shuren, J. E., Schefft, B. K., Yeh, H. S. et al. (1995). Repetition and the arcuate fasciculus. *Journal of Neurology*, *242*(9), 596–8. https://doi.org/10.1007/BF00868813.

Singh, N. C., & Theunissen, F. E. (2003). Modulation spectra of natural sounds and ethological theories of auditory processing. *The Journal of the Acoustical Society of America*, *114*(6), 3394–411. https://doi.org/10.1121/1.1624067.

Sjerps, M. J., Fox, N. P., Johnson, K., & Chang, E. F. (2019). Speaker-normalized sound representations in the human auditory cortex. *Nature Communications*, *10*(1), 2465. https://doi.org/10.1038/s41467-019-10365-z.

Slama, M. C., & Delgutte, B. (2015). Neural coding of sound envelope in reverberant environments. *Journal of Neuroscience, 35*(10), 4452–68. https://doi.org/10.1523/JNEUROSCI.3615-14.2015.

Smith, N. J., & Kutas, M. (2015). Regression-based estimation of ERP waveforms: I. The rERP framework. *Psychophysiology, 52*(2), 157–68. https://doi.org/10.1111/psyp.12317.

Smith, Z. M., Delgutte, B., & Oxenham, A. J. (2002). Chimaeric sounds reveal dichotomies in auditory perception. *Nature, 416*(6876), 87–90. https://doi.org/10.1038/416087a.

Söderström, P., & Cutler, A. (2023). Early neuro-electric indication of lexical match in English spoken-word recognition. *PLoS One, 18*(5), e0285286. https://doi.org/10.1371/journal.pone.0285286.

Söderström, P., Horne, M., & Roll, M. (2017). Stem tones pre-activate suffixes in the brain. *Journal of Psycholinguistic Research, 46*(2), 271–80. https://doi.org/10.1007/s10936-016-9434-2.

Söderström, P., Horne, M., Frid, J., & Roll, M. (2016). Pre-activation negativity (PrAN) in brain potentials to unfolding words. *Frontiers in Human Neuroscience, 10*. https://doi.org/10.3389/fnhum.2016.00512.

Söderström, P., Horne, M., Mannfolk, P., van Westen, D., & Roll, M. (2017). Tone-grammar association within words: Concurrent ERP and fMRI show rapid neural pre-activation and involvement of left inferior frontal gyrus in pseudoword processing. *Brain and Language, 174*, 119–26. https://doi.org/10.1016/j.bandl.2017.08.004.

Söderström, P., Lulaci, T., & Roll, M. (2023). *The Role of Tone in Swedish Speech Segmentation*. Paper presented at the Neurolinguistics in Sweden Conference (NLS 2023).

Sohoglu, E., & Davis, M. H. (2016). Perceptual learning of degraded speech by minimizing prediction error. *Proceedings of the National Academy of Sciences, 113*(12), E1747–56. https://doi.org/10.1073/pnas.1523266113.

Sohoglu, E., Peelle, J. E., Carlyon, R. P., & Davis, M. H. (2012). Predictive top-down integration of prior knowledge during speech perception. *Journal of Neuroscience, 32*(25), 8443. https://doi.org/10.1523/JNEUROSCI.5069-11.2012.

Spratling, M. W. (2008). Predictive coding as a model of biased competition in visual attention. *Vision Research, 48*(12), 1391–408. https://doi.org/10.1016/j.visres.2008.03.009.

Srinivasan, R., Nunez, P. L., Tucker, D. M., Silberstein, R. B., & Cadusch, P. J. (1996). Spatial sampling and filtering of EEG with spline laplacians to estimate cortical potentials. *Brain Topography, 8*(4), 355–66. https://doi.org/10.1007/BF01186911.

Starr, A., McPherson, D., Patterson, J. et al. (1991). Absence of both auditory evoked potentials and auditory percepts dependent on timing cues. *Brain, 114* (3), 1157–80. https://doi.org/10.1093/brain/114.3.1157.

Steinhauer, K., & Drury, J. E. (2012). On the early left-anterior negativity (ELAN) in syntax studies. *Brain and Language, 120*(2), 135–62. https://doi.org/10.1016/j.bandl.2011.07.001.

Steinschneider, M., Nourski, K. V., Kawasaki, H. et al. (2011). Intracranial study of speech-elicited activity on the human posterolateral superior temporal gyrus. *Cerebral Cortex, 21*(10), 2332–47. https://doi.org/10.1093/cercor/bhr014.

Stevens, K. N. (1980). Acoustic correlates of some phonetic categories. *The Journal of the Acoustical Society of America, 68*(3), 836–42. https://doi.org/10.1121/1.384823.

Stevens, K. N., & Blumstein, S. E. (1978). Invariant cues for place of articulation in stop consonants. *The Journal of the Acoustical Society of America, 64* (5), 1358–68. https://doi.org/10.1121/1.382102.

Stivers, T., Enfield, N. J., Brown, P. et al.(2009). Universals and cultural variation in turn-taking in conversation. *Proceedings of the National Academy of Sciences, 106*(26), 10587–92. https://doi.org/10.1073/pnas.0903616106.

Studdert-Kennedy, M. (1987). The phoneme as a perceptuomotor structure. In *Language Perception and Production: Relationships between Listening, Speaking, Reading and Writing.* (pp. 67–84). San Diego: Academic Press.

Suga, N. (1995). Sharpening of frequency tuning by inhibition in the central auditory system: Tribute to Yasuji Katsuki. *Neuroscience Research, 21*(4), 287–99. https://doi.org/10.1016/0168-0102(94)00868-g.

Suga, N. (2008). Role of corticofugal feedback in hearing. *Journal of Comparative Physiology A: Neuroethology, Sensory, Neural, and Behavioral Physiology, 194*(2), 169–83. https://doi.org/10.1007/s00359-007-0274-2.

Summerfield, Q. (1981). Articulatory rate and perceptual constancy in phonetic perception. *Journal of Experimental Psychology: Human Perception and Performance, 7*(5), 1074–95. https://doi.org/10.1037/0096-1523.7.5.1074.

Suomi, K., McQueen, J. M., & Cutler, A. (1997). Vowel harmony and speech segmentation in Finnish. *Journal of Memory and Language, 36*(3), 422–44. https://doi.org/10.1006/jmla.1996.2495.

Taranda, J., Maison, S. F., Ballestero, J. A. et al.(2009). A point mutation in the hair cell nicotinic cholinergic receptor prolongs cochlear inhibition and enhances noise protection. *PLOS Biology, 7*(1), 0071–83, e18. https://doi.org/10.1371/journal.pbio.1000018.

Tervaniemi, M., & Hugdahl, K. (2003). Lateralization of auditory-cortex functions. *Brain Research Reviews*, *43*(3), 231–46. https://doi.org/10.1016/j.brainresrev.2003.08.004.

Tobia, M. J., Iacovella, V., Davis, B., & Hasson, U. (2012). Neural systems mediating recognition of changes in statistical regularities. *Neuroimage*, *63*(3), 1730–42. https://doi.org/10.1016/j.neuroimage.2012.08.017.

Town, S. M., Wood, K. C., & Bizley, J. K. (2018). Sound identity is represented robustly in auditory cortex during perceptual constancy. *Nature Communications*, *9*(1), 4786. https://doi.org/10.1038/s41467-018-07237-3.

Tremblay, P., Baroni, M., & Hasson, U. (2013). Processing of speech and non-speech sounds in the supratemporal plane: Auditory input preference does not predict sensitivity to statistical structure. *Neuroimage*, *66*, 318–32. https://doi.org/10.1016/j.neuroimage.2012.10.055.

Tzourio, N., Massioui, F. E., Crivello, F. et al. (1997). Functional anatomy of human auditory attention studied with PET. *Neuroimage*, *5*(1), 63–77. https://doi.org/10.1006/nimg.1996.0252.

Ulanovsky, N., Las, L., & Nelken, I. (2003). Processing of low-probability sounds by cortical neurons. *Nature Neuroscience*, *6*(4), 391–98. https://doi.org/10.1038/nn1032.

Ungerleider, L. G., & Mishkin, M. (1982). Two cortical visual systems. In D. J. Ingle, M. A. Goodale, & R. J. W. Mansfield (Eds.), *Analysis of Visual Behavior* (pp. 549–86). Cambridge, MA: MIT Press.

Uppenkamp, S., Johnsrude, I. S., Norris, D., Marslen-Wilson, W. D., & Patterson, R. D. (2006). Locating the initial stages of speech-sound processing in human temporal cortex. *Neuroimage*, *31*(3), 1284–96. https://doi.org/10.1016/j.neuroimage.2006.01.004.

Vaughan-Evans, A., Kuipers, J. R., Thierry, G., & Jones, M. W. (2014). Anomalous transfer of syntax between languages. *The Journal of Neuroscience*, *34*(24), 8333. https://doi.org/10.1523/JNEUROSCI.0665-14.2014.

Wacongne, C., Labyt, E., van Wassenhove, V. et al.(2011). Evidence for a hierarchy of predictions and prediction errors in human cortex. *Proceedings of the National Academy of Sciences*, *108*(51), 20754–9. https://doi.org/10.1073/pnas.1117807108.

Wagner, A., & Ernestus, M. (2008). Identification of phonemes: Differences between phoneme classes and the effect of class size. *Phonetica*, *65*(1–2), 106–27. https://doi.org/10.1159/000132389.

Walton, J. P., & Burkard, R. (2001). 40 – Neurophysiological manifestations of aging in the peripheral and central auditory nervous system. In P. R. Hof & C. V. Mobbs (Eds.), *Functional Neurobiology of Aging* (pp. 581–95). San Diego: Academic Press.

Walton, J. P., Frisina, R. D., & O'Neill, W. E. (1998). Age-related alteration in processing of temporal sound features in the auditory midbrain of the CBA mouse. *Journal of Neuroscience, 18*(7), 2764–76. https://doi.org/10.1523/jneurosci.18-07-02764.1998.

Wang, Y., Zhang, J., Zou, J., Luo, H., & Ding, N. (2019). Prior knowledge guides speech segregation in human auditory cortex. *Cerebral Cortex, 29*(4), 1561–71. https://doi.org/10.1093/cercor/bhy052.

Warren, J. D., Jennings, A. R., & Griffiths, T. D. (2005). Analysis of the spectral envelope of sounds by the human brain. *Neuroimage, 24*(4), 1052–7. https://doi.org/10.1016/j.neuroimage.2004.10.031.

Warren, R. M. (1970). Perceptual restoration of missing speech sounds. *Science, 167*(3917), 392–3.

Warren, R. M. (1984). Perceptual restoration of obliterated sounds. *Psychological Bulletin, 96*(2), 371–83. https://doi.org/10.1037/0033-2909.96.2.371.

Weedman, D. L., & Ryugo, D. K. (1996a). Projections from auditory cortex to the cochlear nucleus in rats: Synapses on granule cell dendrites. *Journal of Comparative Neurology, 371*(2), 311–24. https://doi.org/10.1002/(SICI)1096-9861(19960722)371:2<311::AID-CNE10>3.0.CO;2-V.

Weedman, D. L., & Ryugo, D. K. (1996b). Pyramidal cells in primary auditory cortex project to cochlear nucleus in rat. *Brain Research, 706*(1), 97–102. https://doi.org/10.1016/0006-8993(95)01201-X.

Wernicke, C. (1874). *Der aphasische Symptomencomplex: Eine psychologische Studie auf anatomischer Basis*. Breslau: Max Cohn & Weigert.

West, P. (1999). Perception of distributed coarticulatory properties of English /l/ and /r. *Journal of Phonetics, 27*(4), 405–26. https://doi.org/10.1006/jpho.1999.0102.

Whalen, D. H. (1990). Coarticulation is largely planned. *Journal of Phonetics, 18*(1), 3–35. https://doi.org/10.1016/S0095-4470(19)3356-0.

Whitaker, H. A., & Etlinger, S. C. (1993). Theodor Meynert's contribution to classical 19th century aphasia studies. *Brain and Language, 45*(4), 560–71. https://doi.org/10.1006/brln.1993.1060.

Willems, R. M., Frank, S. L., Nijhof, A. D., Hagoort, P., & van den Bosch, A. (2016). Prediction during natural language comprehension. *Cerebral Cortex, 26*(6), 2506–16. https://doi.org/10.1093/cercor/bhv075.

Winer, J. A., Chernock, M. L., Larue, D. T., & Cheung, S. W. (2002). Descending projections to the inferior colliculus from the posterior thalamus and the auditory cortex in rat, cat, and monkey. *Hearing Research, 168*(1–2), 181–95. https://doi.org/10.1016/s0378-5955(02)00489-6.

Wood, C. C. (1976). Discriminability, response bias, and phoneme categories in discrimination of voice onset time. *The Journal of the Acoustical Society of America, 60*(6), 1381–9. https://doi.org/10.1121/1.381231.

Worden, F. G., & Marsh, J. T. (1968). Frequency-following (microphonic-like) neural responses evoked by sound. *Electroencephalography and Clinical Neurophysiology, 25*(1), 42–52. https://doi.org/10.1016/0013-4694(68) 90085-0.

Yin, P., Johnson, J. S., O'Connor, K. N., & Sutter, M. L. (2011). Coding of amplitude modulation in primary auditory cortex. *Journal of Neurophysiology, 105*(2), 582–600. https://doi.org/10.1152/jn.00621.2010.

Young, E. D. (2008). Neural representation of spectral and temporal information in speech. *Philosophical Transactions of the Royal Society B: Biological Sciences, 363*(1493), 923–45. https://doi.org/10.1098/rstb.2007.2151.

Young, E. D., & Sachs, M. B. (1979). Representation of steady-state vowels in the temporal aspects of the discharge patterns of populations of auditory-nerve fibers. *The Journal of the Acoustical Society of America, 66* (5), 1381–403. https://doi.org/10.1121/1.383532.

Yu, A. C., & Lee, H. (2014). The stability of perceptual compensation for coarticulation within and across individuals: A cross-validation study. *The Journal of the Acoustical Society of America, 136*(1), 382–8. https://doi.org/ 10.1121/1.4883380.

Zachlod, D., Rüttgers, B., Bludau, S. et al. (2020). Four new cytoarchitectonic areas surrounding the primary and early auditory cortex in human brains. *Cortex, 128*, 1–21. https://doi.org/10.1016/j.cortex.2020.02.021.

Zatorre, R. J. (1997). Cerebral correlates of human auditory processing. In J. Syka (Ed.), *Acoustical Signal Processing in the Central Auditory System* (pp. 453–68). Boston: Springer US.

Zeng, F.-G., Kong, Y.-Y., Michalewski, H. J., & Starr, A. (2005). Perceptual consequences of disrupted auditory nerve activity. *Journal of Neurophysiology, 93*(6), 3050–63. https://doi.org/10.1152/jn.00985.2004.

Cambridge Elements ☰

Phonetics

David Deterding
Universiti Brunei Darussalam

David Deterding is a Professor at Universiti Brunei Darussalam. His research has involved the measurement of rhythm, description of the pronunciation of English in Singapore, Brunei and China, and the phonetics of Austronesian languages such as Malay, Brunei Malay, and Dusun.

About the Series
The Cambridge Elements in Phonetics series will generate a range of high-quality scholarly works, offering researchers and students authoritative accounts of current knowledge and research in the various fields of phonetics. In addition, the series will provide detailed descriptions of research into the pronunciation of a range of languages and language varieties. There will be Elements describing the phonetics of the major languages of the world, such as French, German, Chinese and Malay as well as the pronunciation of endangered languages, thus providing a valuable resource for documenting and preserving them.

Cambridge Elements ☰

Phonetics

Elements in the Series

Printed in the United States
by Baker & Taylor Publisher Services